The
Luxe Trilogy

Prof Dr Mahul Brahma

Forewords by
Professor John Strachan
Dr Bibek Debroy
(Padma Bhushan)

NewDelhi • London

BLUEROSE PUBLISHERS
India | U.K.

Copyright ©Dr Mahul Brahma 2025

All rights reserved by author. No part of this publication may be reproduced, stored in a retrieval system or transmitted in any form or by any means, electronic, mechanical, photocopying, recording or otherwise, without the prior permission of the author. Although every precaution has been taken to verify the accuracy of the information contained herein, the publisher assumes no responsibility for any errors or omissions. No liability is assumed for damages that may result from the use of information contained within.

BlueRose Publishers takes no responsibility for any damages, losses, or liabilities that may arise from the use or misuse of the information, products, or services provided in this publication.

For permissions requests or inquiries regarding this publication, please contact:

BLUEROSE PUBLISHERS
www.BlueRoseONE.com
info@bluerosepublishers.com
+91 8882 898 898
+4407342408967

ISBN: 978-93-7018-585-2

Cover design: Mrs Sabiya Sinha Roy Brahma
Cover photograph: Mr Indranil Bhoumik
Typesetting: Namrata Saini

First Edition: May 2025

"If there is one person who is eminently qualified to write about luxury, it is Mahul."

— *Padma Bhushan Dr Bibek Debroy, Economist, Author & Former Chairman, PM Economic Advisory Council*

"I wish Mahul's book all the success."

— *Ratan N. Tata*

"Wishing Mahul all the success in all that he endeavours."

— *Amitabh Bachchan*

"This book a culmination of a series of insightful and persuasive mediations on our culture and I wish it very well."

— *Professor John Strachan, Pro Vice Chancellor, Bath Spa University, UK*

Acknowledgement

Dear Reader,

I thank you for your trust in this humble storyteller for allowing me to keep writing and offering my 11th book to you.

I will always be grateful to Bibek da (Debroy), Padma Bhushan, Economist, Author and Former Chairman of Economic Advisory Council to the Prime Minister, for his support and encouragement. The trilogy is dedicated to him. You will always be an inspiration.

Thanks to Mr Ratan Tata and Mr Amitabh Bachchan for your kind words and support.

For his support and encouragement, a special thanks to my dear friend Professor John Strachan, Pro Vice Chancellor, Bath Spa University, UK.

Thanks to Chancellor Sharanjit Leyl and Vice Chancellor Professor Georgina Andrews of Bath Spa University and to Dr Diana Reader and Polly Derbyshire of Bath Business School for their support.

Thanks to Mr Miraj D Shah, Vice Chairman-Governing Body of The Bhawanipur Education Society College and Mr Cecil Antony, Chief Mentor of NSHM.

Thanks to my dear friends, rather younger brothers, Dr Ketan Chokshi and Jatin Chokshi, Managing Directors of Narayan Jewellers, for their support and for sharing insights into the luxury industry.

Thanks to Mr TV Narendran, MD of Tata Steel, Dr Sanjiv Goenka, Chairman of RP-SG Group and Dr Harshavardhan

Neotia, Chairman, AmbujaNeotia Group for their kind support.

Thanks to all the people, publications, organisations and institutions, which have supported me in this journey spanning over two decades with hundreds of columns and 11 books as an author, academic leader, luxury commentator, columnist, communications leader, brand custodian, and editor-in-chief.

Thanks to my family and better half Sabiya for her love, support and encouragement.

May the blessings of Baba Lokenath shower on you!

To Bibek da...you will always be an inspiration!

For Mahul,
With best wishes,
Bibek Deb
25/9/2019.

Praises for The Luxe Trilogy

"I wish Mahul's book all the success."

- *Ratan N. Tata*

"Wishing Mahul all the success in all that he endeavours."

- *Amitabh Bachchan*

"This book a culmination of a series of insightful and persuasive mediations on our culture and I wish it very well."

- *Professor John Strachan, Pro Vice Chancellor, Bath Spa University, UK*

"If there is one person who is eminently qualified to write about luxury, it is Mahul."

- *Padma Bhushan Dr Bibek Debroy, Economist, Author & Former Chairman of PM Economic Advisory Council*

"Let more writings come through the pen of Mahul."

- *Keshari Nath Tripathi, Hon. Governor of West Bengal (Former)*

"You and your writings always have all my blessings Mahul."

- *Mamata Banerjee, Hon Chief Minister of West Bengal*

"Congratulation and best wishes for your new book, Mahul."

— *Harish Bhat, Author and Brand Custodian, Tata Sons*

"Mahul has been able to bring in new thoughts, ideas and perspectives."

— *Nirvik Singh, Chairman and CEO, GREY Group*

"The romance of luxury has waited long for such a deft rendition of insight and eloquence."

— *Kunal Basu, Author*

"A quiet voice that will have a thundering impact. An essential read."

— *Sarnath Banerjee, Graphic Novelist, Author*

"I love the way Mahul deconstructs the mystical world of luxury with his simple, direct, matter-of-fact lucid style of narration.

— *Arnab Chakraborty, National Director, UN-Empretec Programme for India*

About the author

Prof Dr Mahul Brahma FCES, PhD, D.Litt, DBA is a two-time Sahityakosh Samman-winning author of 11 books. He is a luxury commentator, podcaster, columnist, academician, communication, and brand strategist with over two decades of industry and academic experience. He is a Visiting Research Fellow of Bath Business School, UK, Fellow of the Commercial Education Society of Australia (FCES) and Dean and Professor of NSHM Media School in India. He is a former Professor and Dean and Director at Adamas University in India.

He is a TEDx Speaker on mythic value of luxury. Prof Brahma is an award-winning communications leader, specialising in strategic and crisis communications. He was head of CSR, Corporate Communications and Branding in a Tata group company. He has held several leadership positions in English print media, rising to the level of Editor in Chief.

He is an alumnus of — IIM Calcutta, St Xavier's College (Calcutta), Sri Satya Sai University, MICA (Ahmedabad), University of Calcutta, Bath Spa University, UK, and University of Cambridge - Judge Business School.

He is the author of *Decoding Luxe, Dark Luxe* and *Luxe Inferno*. His fourth book *Quarantined: Love in the Time of Corona* is an anthology of dark love stories and has received wide appreciation. His fifth book is *How to Communicate Strategically in Corporate World*. His sixth book *The Mythic Value of Luxury* is a research-based study of myths and what makes luxury brands stand the test of time. His seventh book *Mostly Missing: Be Silly Be Slow* is based on embracing an unconventional approach to life, shunning speed, and seriousness towards living deeply and being mindful. His eighth book *Aesthetic*

Leadership in Luxury was launched in the UK in the heritage city of Bath. The book is about the critical role played by aesthetics and the dominance of aesthetic leadership in the luxury world and how it becomes a game changer for a brand, especially for Aesthete consumers. *The Quiet Luxe* is his 9th book on the revolution of the phenomenon of quiet luxury. *Bharat: The Luxe Story* is his 10th book and was also launched in the UK. *The Luxe Trilogy* is his 11th book.

He has published hundreds of articles, columns and academic papers on luxury communications and branding, and has delivered lectures on the subject at Bath Spa University (UK), University of Scranton (US), IIM Calcutta, IIM Lucknow, IIT KGP-VGSoM, IIT Roorkee, and national industry bodies such as CII and BCC&i.

He was conferred two honorary Doctor of Literature (D.Litt) in luxury and communications by University of Central America (Bolivia) and California Public University (US). He is the winner of Sahityakosh Samman Award 2022 and 2023, Author of the Year 2022 in Bharatiya Sahitya Mahostsav, winner of Indian Shiksha Award 2023 for Academic Leadership in Higher Education, winner of Global Education Award 2022 for Outstanding Academic Leadership, Corporate Communications Thought Leader of the Year Award 2022, Author of the Year Awards in 2022 (Non-Fiction) and 2021 (Fiction), Crisis Communications Leader of the Year 2021, CSR Leader of the Year Award in 2019, Best Communication Strategist of the Year Award in 2019, Brand Leadership Award in 2017, Ecommerce Communication Leader of the Year Award in 2017, Certificate of Excellence in Corporate Communications 2017 and Young Achiever Award in National Awards for Excellence in Corporate Communications 2016. He is listed among Most Influential PR professionals in India under the age of 40 by leading communications publication Reputation Today.

His short films were selected and screened at prestigious film festivals like Cannes Film Festival. He has acted in several Bengali feature films, including 'Aparajito' by Anik Dutta, a film on Satyajit Ray's making of Pather Panchali.

Prof Brahma is an avid golfer with a single-digit handicap.

Wikipedia: https://en.wikipedia.org/wiki/Mahul_Brahma
Website: www.mahulbrahma.com
https://profmahulbrahma.academia.edu/
Facebook: @AuthorMahul
Twitter: @mahulbrahma
Instagram: @mahulbrahma

About The Luxe Trilogy

The Luxe Trilogy is an authoritative, research-based writings spanning across two decades covered in three distinctive books tracing the journey of luxe from dazzle of the Maharajas to the darkness of the Inferno's nine circles of hell. The essence of the trilogy comes from his writings exploring the various facets of luxury from the perspectives of Sociology, Philosophy, Anthropology, History, and Economics, capturing its evolution in India, that is Bharat. It is the 11th book of luxury commentator and columnist Professor Mahul Brahma, commemorating his journey as a luxury columnist and commentator. The three books take the tale of luxe forward with a heady cocktail of fact and fiction inspired by the history of Bharat but not limited by it to ensure that the reader's journey is never linear, never predictable, never boring. From Cartier's Patiala Necklace with 234.5 carat De Beers diamond to custom-made Louis Vuitton bags for keeping *masalas* to converting Rolls Royce Phantoms to garbage trucks, it captures the centuries-old love affair between the Maharajas and global luxury brands. It captures the role of aesthetics in leadership, especially when the world is moving towards a new-age revolution of quiet luxury. The trilogy narrates a quest for the true meaning of luxe, beyond the myopic 'price tag'. The trilogy was launched in the United Kingdom.

The three books of the trilogy essentially are curated to capture the true essence of luxe. The first book narrates the journey of luxe, starting from its inception, capturing the journey of evolution with the Royalty in Bharat. The second book narrates the rising criticality of aesthetic leadership in luxury, from European fashion giants to technology biggies like Apple, especially on the onset of quiet luxury. The book is a comprehensive narration of the story of aesthetic leadership in luxury along the various strategy contours of art, beauty, design, creativity and of course, aesthetics. The third book charts the journey of luxe through the proverbial nine circles of Dante's Inferno to the Paradiso. The three books while in existence separately, together weaves the complete story of luxe unveiling its true and contemporary meaning.

Foreword

The book you have in your hands - or on your mobile device - has some important and entertaining things to say about Indian life and culture and, indeed, that of the wider society in which we all live. *The Luxe Trilogy* is part of a sustained engagement by Professor Mahul Brahma with consumer culture, branding and luxury, and their deep significance in our modern world.

India, in all of its remarkable variety, a country both traditional and hyper-modern, is a key theme of the book. That said, though Bharat is the main focus of his work in this book, Mahul is engaged in an insightful and persuasive engagement with culture in both the eastern and the western worlds; his is a wide ranging and provocative vision.

As an historian of advertising in the United Kingdom and the Republic of Ireland, I always enjoy reading intelligent and though-provoking work on retail, consumer culture, and marketing, and so I enjoyed engaging with this book. Professor Brahma has, indeed, made the subject of luxe his own. Across a series of short, pithy, and thoughtful books he has engaged in a sustained, thought-provoking and entertaining engagement with the subject of luxury and the way in which it resounds though culture. *The Luxe Trilogy* is no exception to this rule; I greatly enjoyed reading it and I am sure you will too. I wish Professor Mahul Brahma well with it.

Professor John Strachan
(BA, MPhil, DPhil, FRHistS, FRAS, FRSA)

Pro Vice Chancellor, Bath Spa University, UK

Foreword

The word "luxe" means we are talking about luxury. The average person loves luxury, even if the pleasure is vicarious. I remember watching a behavioural experiment in a museum. The museum had a chair and you could pay $10 for the privilege of sitting on it. There weren't too many takers willing to pay $10 for the privilege of sitting on a perfectly ordinary-looking chair. The museum then cordoned off the chair behind some ropes and put up a sign saying, "So and so (a celebrity) sat on this chair." Immediately, there was a queue of people willing to pay the price. The chair had acquired a value that surpassed the price. It had become a luxury item. Thorstein Veblen and John Kenneth Galbraith would have scoffed at such instances of conspicuous consumption. However, "luxe" is a fact of life. The dingiest of barbers will have a sign that proclaims, "De-luxe hair-cutting saloon".

Not all de-luxe is dingy. The use of the word does connote branding and quality. Who better than Dr. Mahul Brahma to educate us about luxe? He has been writing on the subject for decades, and he has now given us *The Luxe Trilogy*. The writing is about the dazzle. It explains to the reader what luxe means, with plenty of examples and anecdotes from the early 1900s. In case it hasn't registered, there is fake or counterfeit deluxe too.

A sub-group, which is used in *The Luxe Trilogy*, is a medley of fact and fiction. Perhaps one can call it *faction*.

If you like luxury and luxe, you will like this book. If not, you are a cynic. I am alluding to the famous Oscar Wilde quote from *Lady Windermere's Fan*: A cynic is "A man who knows the price of everything, and the value of nothing."

We forget what Cecil Graham said in response to Lord Darlington. "And a sentimentalist, my dear Darlington, is a man who sees an absurd value in everything and doesn't know the market price of any single thing." You need to be a sentimentalist to appreciate luxe and this book.

Padma Bhushan Dr Bibek Debroy

Economist, Author & Former Chairman of Economic Advisory Council to the Prime Minister

Contents

Luxe Book 1 1

  Chapter 1: Bharat, A Luxe Story... 3

  Chapter 2: Understanding Consumers of Luxury in Bharat 6

  Chapter 3: Of Masstige and The Great Aspiring Middle Class of Bharat... 11

  Chapter 4: The Quiet Luxury 16

  Chapter 5: How to Communicate Quiet Luxury 21

  Chapter 6: Golden rules for creating luxe aura 23

  Chapter 7: What's ailing the conventional 'Asia Strategy' 26

  Chapter 8: Search for perfect USP in luxury 29

  Chapter 9: Multi-billion-dollar wedding industry in Bharat... 32

  Chapter 10: Trick of making luxe worth your wait........... 35

  Chapter 11: Images luxe conjures.. 38

  Chapter 12: Controversy, thy name is luxe 41

  Chapter 13: Karl and the art of luxury brand legacy......... 44

  Chapter 14: A fake, is a fake, is a fake.................................... 47

  Chapter 15: The Mythic Value of Luxury 50

Luxe Book 2 55

  Lecture delivered in the United Kingdom........................... 63

  Lecture delivered in the United Kingdom........................... 67

  Facets of Leadership... 70

  Role of Visual Communication in Aesthetic Leadership ... 76

  Role of Creativity in Aesthetic Leadership.......................... 80

  Organisational Aesthetics in Luxury Brands...................... 83

  Exclusive Case Study: Aesthetic Leadership in Practice .. 87

Luxe Book 3 91

Part A Luxe Inferno 97
Chapter 1: Love at first sight 98
Chapter 2: The Power 103
Chapter 3: The New Identity 107
Chapter 4: The Clash 113
Chapter 5: To Hell and Back 116
Chapter 6: The Paradiso 119

Part B Perception 125
Chapter 1: Musings of millennial millionaires 127
Chapter 2: Masstige – Luxury of the Masses 130
Chapter 3: Of Flaunters and Bling Economy 133
Chapter 4: Art of Subliminal Marketing 135
Chapter 5: Darkness behind the veil of luxury 138
Chapter 6: Of aspirations and mind games 141
Chapter 7: Discovering facets of Luxe Identity 144
Chapter 8: The Luxe Legacy 147
Chapter 9: Philosophy behind Branding Desire 149

Part C Epilogue 154

Luxe Book 1

About Luxe Book 1

This book captures the essence of Prof Mahul Brahma's *Bharat, A Luxe Story*, which is an authoritative, research-based anthology of essays exploring various facets of luxury from the perspectives of Sociology, Philosophy, Anthropology, History, and Economics, revolving around India, that is Bharat, to find a deeper meaning of luxe beyond the myopic 'price tag'. It is the 10th book of Professor Brahma, commemorating two decades of his journey as a luxury columnist and commentator. It captures the centuries-old love affair between Bharat and global luxury brands. From Cartier's Patiala Necklace with 234.5 carat De Beers diamond to custom-made Louis Vuittons and Rolls Royces, Bharat has been the epicentre of branded luxury. The book traces the evolution of luxury in Bharat with the passage of time and change of perspective of Indians, redefining the mythic value of luxury. It traces the passage of Bharat from the dazzling loud luxury to new-age revolution of quiet luxury. *Bharat, The Luxe Story* was launched in the UK in 2024 by Professor John Strachan, Pro Vice Chancellor, Bath Spa University, UK.

CHAPTER 1

Bharat, A Luxe Story

The luxury market is expected to grow by 2-4% in 2024, with regional and national variations, according to an analysis by McKinsey. Luxury retail is expected to reach at least EUR 305 billion this year due to strong demand in Europe, the US and India, that is Bharat. Local consumption remains important in China.

In Bharat, the love affair between luxury brands and showcasing of luxury reached the pinnacle during the 1920s when India alone was consumer of 20 per cent of global sales of Rolls Royce or when a certain Nizam had 50 Harley Davidsons for his personal messengers or when Zebra-driven phaetons used to give competition to the horse-driven carriages.

Surprised? Picture this: it is estimated that over roughly 200 years, the East India Company and the British Raj siphoned out at least GBP 9.2 trillion (or USD 44.6 trillion, since the exchange rate was USD 4.8 per GBP during much of the colonial period).

In 1926, the Maharaja of Patiala commissioned Cartier, its largest till date, to remodel his crown jewels, which included the 234.69 carat De Beers diamond. The result was a breathtaking Patiala necklace weighing 962.25 carats with 2,930 diamonds.

In 1928, the Maharaja Hari Singh of Jammu and Kashmir placed orders for custom-made 30 trunks from luggage maker Louis Vuitton over a period of six months. In my first book

Decoding Luxe, I have delved a little deeper into the Louis Vuitton trunk story and let me share some more interesting facets of this long and loving courtship of LV with Indian Royalty. Louis Vuitton was unique in use of valuable materials and precious leathers. The luxury house was always able to cater to elaborate special requests from the Indian Maharajahs, no matter how extraordinary, elaborate or detailed the demands were. Maharajah Hari Singh had ordered all the trunks imaginable for the most diverse of items -- golf clubs, turbans, decorations, polo sticks, horseshoes, colonial helmets, among others.

And then there was a trunk containing a desk with first-aid kit, a trunk for files, a desk trunk, two special tilting trunks intended for cleaning shoes, a special monogrammed case for a typewriter, several Deauville and Beauvais suitcases adapted to lunch cases, a dictaphone, and even a semi-rigid canvas casing for a crib, intended for the heir to the throne. All had a very distinctive stamp, 'J & K', with a diagonal stripe, the hot stamp.

Among the purchases of Sayajirao Gaekwad III of Baroda, were a Torino suitcase with toiletry accessories in vermeil and ivory, a shoe trunk, and a tea case. The suitcase with the toiletries kit and tea set was lined with Morocco leather. The toiletries kit consisted of more than fifty items in silver: brushes, bottles, soap boxes, razors, and a jewellery box as well. The trunks and boxes if the Maharaja were covered in Lozine.

Now let's talk about an interesting royalty story of the brand that runs on reputation -- Roll Royce. In my second book *Dark Luxe*, I have shared a great example in the story 'Death of a Phantom' of Maharaja Jai Singh buying the epitome of reputation in Western culture – Rolls Royce, six of them, and converting them into garbage vans for the city. Maharaja Jai

Singh visited London and was wearing casual dress. During his city tour, he spotted the Rolls Royce showroom and entered it to know more about the cars and even buy the vehicle. However, seeing his "native Indian" appearance, the security of the showroom assumed that he is a beggar and did not allow him to enter the showroom. Thus, he purchased and converted all six Rolls Royce cars into garbage collectors for his kingdom. It is as loud as it gets!

Therefore, luxury, especially in the context of royalty in Bharat was never "quiet" or subliminal but always "loud" and on the face. The evolution of luxury in Bharat has seen an elaborate dominance of logos as seen with flaunters.

CHAPTER 2

Understanding Consumers of Luxury in Bharat

The year 2023 has been a challenge for luxury brands globally. The brands have shown resilience, especially in Bharat, and, to its consumers, is more desirable than ever. At a time when the outlook is more challenging, and as customers become more discerning about where, how, and why they spend, luxury brands must ensure they are agile and flexible enough to respond to the uncertainties they face.

While there are some broad alignments between luxury consumers globally, there is a need to have a deeper understanding of price-sensitive and value-for-money seeking luxury consumers in Bharat. They are classified into Flaunters, Connoisseurs, Aesthetes, and Experientialists.

Consumers of Loud Luxury - Flaunters

From the time of the Maharajas, flaunting luxury has been the primary objective of owning luxury and thus visibility of the logo even to an extent that others feel uncomfortable was acceptable and desired. And later with evolution, The Great Indian Aspiring Middle Class (GIAMC) has become an integral part of this category of flaunters.

Cut to today, a socialite friend who used to swear by a clutch that she used to take to every party had secretly confessed that she isn't that fond of it but only carries it for the monogram tag. That's the power of a brand for this genre.

Welcome to the world of flaunters who tend to value brand name over all other factors. The visibility of the brand name at strategic positions across the product is a big deal for them as such purchases denote their status in their society. So, the brand needs to be aspirational, else, what's the big deal? The newly rich or new money classes, especially their younger counterparts, are mostly badge seekers at the stage where the brand name is supposedly the biggest status indicator. There is a strong urge to prove to the society that they are also a part of the elitist luxury brand-wagon.

According to a survey more such consumers were seen in cities like Ludhiana and Raipur where they justify the ownership of brands by stating that they are now in a status or position which makes it de rigueur. Interestingly, for this category of consumers, the brands are on a continuum. They can show off Zara as a daily wear to Prada on special occasions with élan.

As flaunters move up the societal ladder, the badge value is conferred not only by the brand but also by the level of difficulty in obtaining the product or service. Dinner reservation at hard-to-get restaurants, Birkin or Kelly bags for which the wait list is over four years, monogrammed and hot stamped Louis Vuitton bags with their initials, accessories made from exotic leather like of crocodile or snake -- the ability to acquire these with relative ease reflects their status.

To tap this segment of consumers, well known but exclusive services and products are the way forward.

Consumers of Quiet Luxury

The next two categories – Connoisseurs and Aesthetes -- belong a segment of the New Maharajas, the Richie Rich of today, who have replaced the age-old royalty. However, there is a significant difference in the way the showcase their wealth and luxury. They are quiet in terms of displaying logos of luxury brands. These categories of consumers pride themselves in being more knowledgeable in their understanding the luxury brands. They do, however, flaunt but only to the other New Maharajas and not to the masses. They leave subtle indications of the exclusivity that they own so that they can say how special they are, even among specials. *(Reference: The Quiet Luxe by the author)*

Connoisseurs

This genre is passionate in certain areas of interest and is mostly well-informed and knowledgeable about it. These could be art, scotch, wine, watches, writing instruments, cigars, horses, not particularly in that order. These connoisseurs get together and appreciate the finer aspects of their passion. They form clubs and meet for a quiet appreciation of the finer things in life — it may be a Horology Society of timekeepers or a Wine Club or a Cuban Cigar Club or a Super Car Club.

This segment just revels in enjoying what they appreciate the most. For instance, the Single Malt Club members come together, discuss, study, debate and share their appreciation and experience in high spirits (pun intended).

They will spend their time and money in pursuit of the collection of personal passion points. They make the pursuit of their area of passion a mission and pursue it with zest and will not bat an eyelid for spending a fortune on limited editions, or handcrafted editions or spirit of the bygone era.

They are reluctant to place value on brands unless it stands for exquisite exclusivity. They take pride in their knowledge of esoteric brands that are not widely known. Luxury to them is purely a matter of the level of craftsmanship, the number of man hours spent, which will determine the quality of the products or services that they buy. Niche, but specialised brands across categories will make their mark with these consumers. They are willing to pay a higher premium so curated services that bring such products to them will be a great getaway to tap into their need for excellence.

Aesthetes

To this genre, the brand is much less important than the design. Aesthetes are quiet luxury consumers purely because they have arrived at a stage of income due to which they can indulge in their love for design among luxury brands or products.
They will shell out a bomb because the object of desire is hand stitched and not because of the label. They pride themselves for having an eye that picks up the unique and bold in design.

The difference between them and the connoisseur is that the latter has certain passions which they follow with zeal and the quality and craftsmanship are very important. However, for the former category, it is the aesthetic appeal, the look, the intricacies of the design that appeal to their senses. They are also likely to pursue this aesthetic across categories unlike a connoisseur.

Aesthetes and Flaunters are on the opposite ends of the spectrum. While Aesthetes are obsessed with design and label or logo comes quite low on the priority list, while for Flaunters label or logo comes right on top and design takes a backseat. However, even Aesthetes are Flaunters in a way, they also flaunt their exquisite designs and feel pride at the snob quotient that most people are not even able to understand or appreciate the elegance. They feel exclusive.

To tap quiet luxury consumers, luxury brands need to showcase more distinctive and unique designs.

The next category is a very interesting category as it is hard to classify it in terms of loud or quiet luxury. These consumers will prefer foreign holidays to diamond jewellery. A jeweller friend once told me that exotic holidays have become their biggest competition.

The Experientialists

This genre typically values new and exciting experiences, more than buying products or brands. They lavishly spend on experiences. In their structured lives they seek a getaway, hence five-star hotel stays, fine dining or adventurous/thrilling experiences are their poison. Luxury to them brings up images of being suspended in time and space, not having the pressures of daily life and work responsibilities as they enjoy the time away.

The most intriguing part is that the Experientialist consumer may well be an Aesthete when it comes to apparel and accessories, while a Connoisseur in art may be a Flaunter when it comes to automobiles or his home. Indian consumers are yet to reach a stage where their lives are only dominated by luxury brands, and they are constantly evolving.

CHAPTER 3

Of Masstige and The Great Aspiring Middle Class of Bharat

In 1899, the sociologist Thorstein Veblen coined the term conspicuous consumption to explain the spending of money on and the acquiring of luxury commodities (goods and services) specifically as a public display of economic power – the income and the accumulated wealth – of the buyer.

With the rising strength of the middle class, conspicuous consumers in Bharat often buy those goods & services which are too expensive for other classes of society (social status). They buy these expensive items to show that they are a class above or to show their spending power.

Therefore, mixing the right portion of the snob-value is by far the biggest challenge faced by a luxury brand – quiet and loud both. It's not about alienating others, but that exclusive positioning needs to be there. The right portion is the magic potion. More of a co-existence of the presence and the absence of snob quotient, side by side.

You need to have the low-hanging accessories like sunglasses or perfumes or key chains or coin purses or scarves or what have you. This will lure a section of clients who are heavy spenders in premium brand space and are yet to turn big spenders in the luxury space because they are not sure about the return on investment or RoI, as we call it in corporate parlance. For them, these low-hanging fruits are not value for money, but they certainly are value for label. So, they just pay for the logo and are happy as it remains well within their budget and are not frivolous but smart. For them, these spends are a deal, the product may be a key chain or a coin purse but who cares. Logo rules in loud luxe!

Let's move into a more interesting segment: the masses with limited means. Let me first introduce a term masstige to explain this. A portmanteau of the words mass and prestige masstige has been described as "prestige for the masses." The term was popularised by Michael Silverstein and Neil Fiske in their book Trading Up and Harvard Business Review article "Luxury for the Masses." Masstige products are defined as "premium but attainable," having two aspects: (1) They are considered luxury or premium products and (2) They have price points that fill the gap between mid-market and super premium.

Take for instance, in South Korea, Louis Vuitton's Speedy 30 handbag has been nicknamed the three-second bag because it feels like you see one every three seconds. As one of the many entry-level products this has been developed to deliver value for money on a smaller, yet perhaps equally indulgent, taste of the brand narrative. So, entry-level products — accessories, belts, scarfs, wallets, small purses, and the likes — of the luxury brands have a clear demand among this segment. They cater to the need of just flaunting the labels.

Luxury brands extend downwards with these low-hanging, seemingly affordable fruits to whet the appetite of the value-for-label masses.

So, both the Maharaja and the Praja, can flaunt the same labels. Yes, it has taken centuries, but democratisation of luxury has finally happened.

Democratisation has become the great leveller.

The rise of the middle class

In Bharat, the category of the Great Indian Aspiring Middle Class (GIAMC) constitutes the masses with means. It has become a power to reckon with as far as luxury buying is concerned. All the major luxury brands owe their existence to GIAMC. In fact, dear New Maharajas, we brand custodians, would love to say that you are the biggest driver of luxury. However, deep in our hearts we know that it is the Great Indian Aspiring Middle Class, who drives the luxury market in this great nation.

If there is one big purchase of a hot stamped monogram LV trunk, then simultaneously hundreds of monogram belts, monogram small wallet scarfs, bracelets, and the likes fly off the shelves. LV might be reaching one New Maharaja's household, may be for the nth time, but it also reaches hundreds, even thousands of households of the Great Indian Aspiring Middle Class for the first time.

Feeding into the aspiration of millions is masstige. How to keep the aspiration alive still seems to be the biggest challenge. What if the brand loses its exclusivity and elitism in trying to just dip into the mass market? But the raked-up moolah from the sheer volume game is also hard to ignore.

To sell or not to sell (to the masses)? A big question that all luxury brands eternally face.

Many, however, have been able to strike a balance with pricing being the key. The entire process has a few elaborate steps, as I had shared in Decoding Luxe, a patient luxury brand manager once explained to me:

1. Identify your signature products and add a premium to their prices. These are meant to tease the aspirations of the GIAMC, who can't afford them. Mostly display the pictures of these

signature items and make sure they are always out of stock and fresh stock is on the anvil from Germany or France. The GIAMC will keep coming back.

2. Identify special edition, handcrafted pieces of quiet luxury that you want the New Maharajas to buy. These should be on display so that they can look and feel it and then take it home. These have a premium attached due to their exclusivity.

3. And then comes the masstige products to satiate the appetite of the GIAMC for them to flaunt that logo of the brand they always aspired to buy loud luxury.

Interestingly, the luxury brands never advertise their masstige products to the GIAMC. This is a precautionary measure to avoid any visible brand dilution. The targeted class, however, advertises and brands these products to their peers, all for free. So, a strong brand pull is generated with this segment, the aspiration lives on and grows, much to a luxury brand's advantage.

This very aspiration for loud luxe has also led to the creation of a phenomenal market of knock offs and first copies. Let me brief you on the rationale behind spending hard earned money on low quality fakes.

Dear Readers, it is aspiration at play again. Not always is it possible for GIAMC, for example, to buy a scarf for INR 30,000, when with that money he could have bought a piece of jewellery. And what are the chances of that scarf surviving the washing machine or the domestic help's onslaught? At the end of the day, it is a piece of cloth.

This is where the knock off market comes to the rescue. You get a similar scarf for INR 500 and only a trained eye will be able to tell you the difference. If it is torn, replace it with another brand for the same price. The same holds true for belts, small leather goods, coin purses, and the likes. The most interesting part is that you can even aim for a big product, a decent copy, at a fraction of the original price that the GIAMC would have otherwise never been able to own.

The most-replicated brands are most-aspired brands such as Louis Vuitton and Rolex.

Coming back to the tale of the low-hanging affordable fruits of the luxury tree, the Great Indian Middle Class will go out of their way to own a piece of that brand, sleep with it and dream about the bigger signature pieces in the larger-than-life posters at the boutiques that always tease them.

Loud luxury lures the Great Indian Aspiring Middle Class like a seductress.

CHAPTER 4

The Quiet Luxury

Quiet luxury is a minimalist approach to luxury and fashion that emphasises timeless elegance, legacy, aesthetics, subliminal ego and exclusivity. Imagine spending INR 2 lakh on a jacket that is not adorned all over with logo of Gucci or Louis Vuitton. So, people will not be able to even identify that it is a luxury spend. It will not make any noise. So, what's the point?

However, your jacket is a subtle cut that you jacket has that is a signature of a certain elite tailor at Savile Row. Let me elaborate a bit. Savile Row is a street in Mayfair, central London, which is principally known for traditional bespoke tailoring for men.

Wikipedia says that tailors started doing business in the area in the late 18th century; first in Cork Street, about 1790, then by 1803 in Savile Row itself. In 1846, Henry Poole, later credited as the creator of the dinner jacket, opened an entrance to Savile Row from his tailoring premises in Old Burlington Street. Founded in 1849 by Henry Huntsman, H. Huntsman & Sons moved to No. 11 Savile Row with the ending of the war in 1919. During First World War, Huntsman's was a tailor to the military, producing dress uniforms for British officers. In 1969, Nutters of Savile Row modernised the style and approach of traditional Savile Row tailoring; a modernisation that continued into the 1990s with the 'New Bespoke Movement', involving the designers Richard James, Ozwald Boateng, and Timothy Everest. The term 'bespoke' as applied to fine tailoring is understood to have originated in Savile Row and came to mean a suit cut and made by hand.

So, coming back to your jacket, it is thus a hand-stitched bespoke from Savile Row. Thus, it is luxury. However, only someone who also is a regular with Savile Row will be able to identify what you are wearing. So, you are crowding out the Great Indian Aspiring Middle Class as well as the Nouveau Riche or "New Money" segment of New Maharajas to only extend your vanity to the "Old Money" New Maharajas. So, your "quiet flaunting" luxury is exclusively for only those who are a class above others. Quiet luxury is new-age minimalism, with a larger focus on investment pieces and thoughtful shopping habits.

Thus comes the Aesthetes and Connoisseurs as explained in the earlier chapters.

Here, it is so exclusive that even if you have the means, you are not invited. Exclusivity and ego are the two main drivers of quiet luxury.

An Indian example of quiet luxury is the Shahtoosh shawl, woven from the fur of a rare Tibetan antelope, which is on the verge of extinction. It is crafted over years and only a connoisseur can identify a Shahtoosh and its luxury quotient. When a Shahtoosh shawl is compared with a logo-studded Gucci or LV scarf, it becomes easy to discern between quiet and loud luxury. *(Reference: The Quiet Luxe by author)*

Ego and Exclusivity

Not humility but ego creates quiet luxury brands, makes them reach the stars. As Sherlock Holmes once said, "My dear Watson, I cannot agree with those who rank modesty among the virtues".

But false ego can put you down and crush you. So, your brand has to be worth it.

Rolls Royce once run an ad where the car did not have a fuel tank. The arrogant tagline, as I had mentioned earlier, said: "A car that runs on reputation".

For a quiet luxury brand, being humble never pays, it's all about being special or exclusive. The brand should be able to dazzle quietly, to stand out in the crowd.

A marketer tries to sell an exclusivity quotient, so when you showcase a particular label, you at least notionally belong to an exclusive club, like a Savile Row Club.

The arrogance that comes from prohibitive pricing to crowd out clients, makes a brand aspirational. When Rolex says "Live for greatness" it is not talking about the product, or the patented perpetual movement, or the oyster casing, or the brilliant design, it is talking about an aspiration. You are entering the exclusive league of greats like JFK or of Martin Luther King Jr and the likes. Being a masculine brand always, Rolex has been able to develop and nurture male ego over decades, and this has proved instrumental for the company's success and it is still revelling in that glory. In a way the brand is selling legacy, a life of greatness, a masculine ego that stands distinguished.

Another example is Louis Vuitton. "There are journeys that turn into legends," when LV used this tagline for Sean Connery during its core values campaign, it was not selling the classic keep-all travel bag. It was selling a story of a great legendary travel, and that too with a legend. The pieces showcased in that series were very selectively chosen and out of character for a brand that is known for loud luxury. This was a classis quiet luxury campaign by LV.

The art is in not only selling the inclusion but more so selling the exclusion.

India's noted graphic novelist and my friend Sarnath Banerjee (author of Corridor and All Quiet in Vikaspuri) in a story, has captured the essence of this "exclusion principle", albeit in his own comic panache. There are customers who walk in and quickly check a few models and close the buy. However, there are others who come down to check out an expensive car like a Rolls Royce or a Jaguar but is not sure whether it is worth that premium. This kind is more for an economical car with a better mileage, but the legacy factor still haunts them. The car salesman instead of hard selling, brilliantly captures this dilemma and thereby hangs a tale. The salesman very cleverly says that these luxury cars are not for "people like you and I" who will prefer more value for their money and not invest in such "esoteric and intangible" notions of legacy. Needless to say, after four-five such examples of "people like you are I" the deal is closed. The legacy wins again and so do the aspiration.

Ironically, we all are in the same queue, waiting eagerly to be treated as special. The "exclusion principle" works like magic.

Legacy is an integral part of quiet luxury. Stroking the aspiration to be a part of legacy is a strategy that quiet luxury brands use in tapping into the potential customers. They are intrigued at the differential treatment doled out to them by the boutique managers for not being a part of its existing esteem clientele. The potential clients are never ignored but they are subtly sent the message that "you also can become a part of this elite treatment and legacy if you use your cash or card a little more generously". This exclusion principle makes these clients with means, feel intrigued and dejected. In comes "greatness" and "legacy" to the rescue. The deal then is no more only value for money but also "totally worth it".

And "for people like you and I" who doesn't have the means, keep aspiring and writing about the legacy. With just a swipe, the Legacy is you to keep.

So New Maharajas it is always a choice to be classified as old money or new money, that is, to join the quiet luxury club or the loud luxury club. Therefore, the selection of the brands as well as products will define the way ahead.

CHAPTER 5

How to Communicate Quiet Luxury

The way to communicate "loud luxury" or luxury where overt showcasing is the primary objective to consumers who are flaunters or who basically are logo-driven consumers is always selling logos and more logos.

But how do we communicate "quiet luxury" or luxury where the voice of logo is muted and the ego fight is on subliminal flaunting of luxury? Quiet luxury is a minimalist approach to luxury and fashion that emphasises timeless elegance, legacy, aesthetics, subliminal ego and exclusivity.

Let's first understand the consumers of quiet luxury, primarily the ones who are obsessed with aesthetics such as Aesthetes and the ones who are the "real collectors" or rather the Connoisseurs. These are the two categories where the consumer is just not swayed by logos.

These are consumers who come from "old money", who do not feel the need to establish the "coming of age" to everyone. However, they are more ego-driven to establish their supremacy to the others who they think are also from the same strata of society. The subtle cut of the bespoke suit from Savile Row or the logo-less uber-class limited edition jacket of Louis Vuitton, which are hard to find but the trained eye will know that it is 10 times more expensive than the logo-studded jacket are the signs of flaunting in "quiet luxury" space.

So communication also must be bespoke. Communication must be driven by two factors – exclusivity and ego. Therefore, luxury brands who are targeting the quiet luxury consumers have to keep a special communications and branding package ready wherein the logo is not showcased but the exclusivity is.

You can buy the logo but you can't just buy the class!

Luxury leather brand Bottega Veneta has no logo as it says the consumer is the biggest brand. An expert eye can tell from a distance from Bottega's signature "intreciatto" weaving craftsmanship. So, you must communicate the ego-booster – "you are the biggest brand".

We are all waiting eagerly to be treated as special.

Brand communication needs to explicitly showcase exclusivity, the legacy of the brand, the intricacies of the movements in case of a watch or of the craftsmanship in other cases…harping on the number of man hours that have been painstakingly spent to make this unique piece as a "quiet luxury" desirable product.

Communication becomes complicated when the same brand appeals to both consumers of loud and quiet luxury. The biggest challenge is that the old money brands and the new money brands seldom overlap. Brands like Gucci and Louis Vuitton are more known to appeal to loud luxury consumers or the flaunters while Patek Philippe appeals more to quiet luxury consumers such as the Connoisseurs and Aesthetes. So, for Louis Vuitton or Gucci to appeal to old money consumers the brand messaging needs to abruptly change and appeal to exclusivity and subliminal ego boosting for an effective brand communication.

So, to communicate quiet luxury a brand needs to know the art of subliminal marketing wherein the ego, legacy, exclusivity, man-hour investment and, of course, the story are the key drivers.

CHAPTER 6

Golden rules for creating luxe aura

Bespoke product offerings and exclusive limited editions are just half of the picture, and in 2024, the focus is on individuality and exclusivity in every sense whilst placing the customer in control.

The multi-billion-dollar question that worries every brand custodian is – what is the right strategy to brand a luxury product or service? Let us see how luxury branding is different, and take you through the golden rules that need to be followed to make a luxury product or service withstand the test of time.

These tenets are:

1. Selling legacy

2. Creating aspiration

3. Creating exclusivity

4. Customisation

5. Understanding the history and culture of target geography

6. EMOD - Every point of contact needs to be trained well to handle customers

7. Keeping brand promise

8. Making the 'haves' feel special

9. Never forgetting the have-nots

10. Targeted marketing and communicating of luxe stories

When a Rolex advertisement showcases that the legendary US President JFK used to sport the watch, it sends a message to the target customers – you are a part of legacy. Brands like Louis Vuitton, Rolex, IWC and Montblanc have been successfully harnessing this "legacy quotient" to get more and more customers. These watches or writing instruments or luggage crafters charge a hefty premium because of the legacy quotient, which just money can't buy. You must be worth it. It is a very smart strategy to establish aspiration, which creates a pull towards a product or service – something that's beyond the price tag and dazzles you. It is critical for a brand to evoke aspiration, which, like legacy, gives a sense of exclusivity. A brand custodian needs to keep this key element in mind while crafting the brand story. It is this sense of being a part of an elite group that lures buyers and makes them loosen their purse strings. If by buying a luxury product or service a customer gets a feeling that only money is the differential factor, then he or she will feel insecure that anyone will be allowed in this so-called 'exclusive club' if they have the moolah. This feeling of exclusivity creates loyalty.

In today's global village, every brand is looking at new and potent geographies such as India or China. It is imperative to start customising their offerings for these financially significant markets. While ad-hoc efforts are made, there is no structured strategy in place to effectively tap these markets. The need of the hour is to develop a deeper understanding of the history and culture of these geographies.

A key element that makes a luxury brand work wonders is EMOD, or Every Moment of Discipline. Every touchpoint needs to be properly trained to handle clients. Customer experience is a key element that generates loyalty. A call centre executive or a store attendant can significantly contribute towards gaining a customer or losing him or her for good, generating good or bad publicity in the process. This is a critical area, especially in the age of social media.

From a brand's perspective, the most important golden rule is to keep your promise made to the customer. It is sacrosanct and under no circumstance can it be compromised, otherwise the integrity of the brand comes into question.

While luxury brands need to make their Richie Rich customers or "haves" feel exclusive and pampered, a close eye must be kept on the masses that keep the coffers filled. The sheer volume of masstige sale helps every luxury brand worth its salt show the rosy numbers. While the big-ticket purchases are very important, the smaller-ticket buys make magic. So, maintain a fine balance between the haves and the have-nots.

Finally, luxury branding is all about telling stories. The right mix of targeted marketing and communication of these brand stories create aspiration in the eyes of the customers.

By combining physical elements with digital content, luxury brands can immerse their customers in a memorable and shareable experience that instantly brings their products to life. Interactive packaging will become a prominent trend in 2024.

CHAPTER 7

What's ailing the conventional 'Asia Strategy'

Revenue in the luxury goods market amounts to USD56.08 billion in 2024. The market is expected to grow annually by 3.92% (CAGR 2024-2028). The market's largest segment is the segment luxury watches & jewellery with a market volume of USD25.25 billion in 2024.

For brands looking to break into the Chinese luxury market, the rules are changing. Understanding cultural idiosyncrasies, adapting to changing consumer tastes and embracing the experience economy are just some of the strategies for success. But understanding these dynamics isn't a luxury – it's a necessity.

Luxury brands globally always make the mistake of having a so-called overall "Asia Strategy", which primarily involves two countries that are different in more ways than one. These two countries, India and China, have historically been very diverse in demonstrating their opulence and even today, they represent very different categories of luxury brand consumers. Let me elaborate with a bit of historical perspective.

India, as is evident from the examples in earlier chapters, has a rich legacy of using luxury since the inception of these international brands, unlike China. The prosperous community, even the royalty in China, have been closed and heavily dependent on exquisite local products. The pride of "made in China" to the wealthy locals was a Great Wall that barred the entry of foreign luxury brands.

In India, the scenario took a 180-degree turn post-Independence and anything remotely opulent was frowned upon. It's only in the past few decades that there has been a shift, and the 'New Maharajas' – industrialists, entrepreneurs, professionals and the rural rich – started blatantly adoring and flaunting all things luxurious.

Another very strong category of luxury consumers in India is the great Indian middle class. The monogrammed Louis Vuitton products might be reaching a New Maharaja's household time and again, but they also reach hundreds of households in the great aspiring middle class for the first time.

However, the Chinese market is not dominated by either of these above categories. The new-found growth in the luxury sector is fuelled only by the new, young, upper-middle class with a tendency to spend rather than save. They are the new-generation, first-time customers for luxury products. In China, the 'New Maharajas' are averse to 'foreign' luxury brands; the middle class is rising as a consumer but has not been able to make a mark yet in the top lines of these brands.

Unfortunately, despite these marked differences, international luxury brands still find it convenient to have a common overall strategy for consumers in India and China. This a strategically wrong.

The approach of these luxury giants is very ad-hoc and clearly lacks a comprehensive and cohesive strategy. For example, you will suddenly see a slew of products launched to commemorate the Chinese New Year. Similar efforts will be made to cash in on celebrations like Diwali in India. There have been sporadic efforts too, like Hermes deciding to suddenly come up with an expensive saree, out of the blue.

If the strategic objective is to get a significant pie of the markets in China or India, or for that matter anywhere in the globe, the first thing these brands need to do is to understand the intrinsic nature of the consumers. The best way to know that is by customer immersion, understanding their traditions with a historical perspective.

It becomes easy to put together a comprehensive strategy towards creating an aspiration for the brand and converting these buyers as loyal customers once there is complete clarity on the evolution of the luxury consumer in a given geography.

It's time to wipe clean the overall 'Asia Strategy' and replace it with strategies for specific geographies with a deeper understanding of their traditions, culture and history.

CHAPTER 8

Search for perfect USP in luxury

USP or Unique Selling Proposition is the factor that makes a product or service "different" and "better" than that of their competitors. Theodore Levitt, a professor at Harvard Business School, said, "Differentiation is one of the most important strategic and tactical activities in which companies must constantly engage."

The issue is how can a brand custodian frame a proposition which is unique and will compel the customers to be loyal to your brand, or tempting as it sounds, switch their loyalty away from the competition?

USP is even more critical in luxury marketing because of the premium that these brands charge. It plays a key role in justifying the value for money for price-sensitive Indian customers. In luxury, the choice of USP becomes a critical exercise as there may even be a case when the strongest element of the brand may not necessarily be unique to it. While the brand needs to strategically focus on its strength, it may have to focus on some other element for defining its USP.

Let us consider a watch brand. Its USP or core strength cannot be that it is Swiss made. The competition has been exploiting it since time immemorial. Rolex, a watch with core strength of patented complications and movements can use this as far as its strategy charting is concerned. However, its USP can't be this patent because all its competitors have some movement or complication patented. Therefore, Rolex creates a USP with its campaign "Live for Greatness" using great leaders such as JFK and Martin Luther King Jr.

Another watch, which is priced way higher than Rolex, is Patek Phillippe. Unlike most be-jewelled high-end Rolex models, Patek Phillippe has a very traditional handcrafted design. Its USP, as stated in its most popular campaign, is "You never actually own a Patek Philippe. You merely look after it for the next generation." This beautiful campaign, primarily with father and son duos, established in the minds of customers that this watch deserves to be expensive as it transcends generations. Even in this case, Patek's core strength lies in its patented movements and complications.

The unique selling proposition creates differentiation in the minds of customers, making them prefer one brand over the other, irrespective of the fact that both of them are Swiss-made with patented movements and complications.

"There are journeys that turn into legends" was a very impactful "Core Values" campaign by Louis Vuitton where the brand was able to create its USP, keeping its competition far behind, with names like Sir Sean Connery. This USP conjures the image of icons using Louis Vuitton bags in their legendary journey, luring the customers into becoming a part of that imagery. The core strength, which will strategically be the key to LV, would, however, be something else – such as the quality of its canvas or its Damier signature design.

The unique selling proposition is also intricately related to another very critical concept for luxury brands – positioning. This refers to the space that a brand occupies in the customers' minds and how it is distinguished from the products of the competitors. Originally, positioning focused on the product and with Ries and Trout, grew to include building a product's reputation and ranking among competitor's products. USP is typically what you think is your uniqueness for selling your product or service, whereas positioning is what your target audience thinks of you. While a brand needs to focus on its

USP, it is imperative that an outside-in approach is simultaneously taken to understand what the audience perceives as its differentiator.

Gucci's USP is their unique craftsmanship. Going by the records, the top three Gucci items explored by shoppers online are flip-flops, shoes, and belts. With a brand value of USD 12.7 billion, Gucci is one of the richest brands in the fashion world.

LVMH's commitment to exceptional craftsmanship and quality sets it apart from competitors. Employing skilled artisans and using high-quality materials, Louis Vuitton ensures that each product meets its exacting standards, further enhancing its reputation and customer loyalty.

So, every brand custodian must consider both the inside-out as well as outside-in approaches while crafting the unique selling proposition for a luxury brand.

CHAPTER 9

Multi-billion-dollar wedding industry in Bharat

Survey conducted by the Confederation of All India Traders (Cait) Research & Trade Development Society estimates a flow of about INR4.25 trillion in wedding-related purchases and services. More than 3.5 million weddings are expected to take place between November 23 and December 15, 2023, in Bharat.

In Bharat, beside monsoon, the only season that is here to stay in that of weddings. And small wonder, amid the slew of celebrity marriages, the cacophony hit crescendo with the Ambani wedding. While the events were dripping wealth, there was a dominance of traditional Indian labels and non-labels, which exuded luxury by their sheer presence. Conspicuously missing were the international luxury labels, which have managed to become an integral part of the daily lives of these stakeholders but remain somewhat amiss in one of the most important days of their lives – the big fat Indian wedding. Let's explore why these international luxury brands been so shy in getting a pie of this multi-billion-dollar wedding market in India?

First, we must identify the missing ingredient. And to know the missing ingredient, we must understand the ethos of an Indian wedding. The root lies in our traditions. What the wedding showcases is the celebration of the traditions in the most authentic way, making ample room to showcase opulence and luxe. Billions of dollars are mostly spent on non-international luxury brands to make sure that the heady mix of splurge and tradition is maintained.

The key lies in a deeper understanding of the Indian traditions and then customising the products to suit the occasion. Arrogance and pride for their craft and market have historically prevented international luxury brands from customisation for a certain geography. Much later, many of them realised business is more important than pride and so they started coming with customised collections which are geography-specific, especially for the two largest markets – India and China.

For example, to celebrate the Chinese Lunar New Year, Giorgio Armani's collection had dominance of the colour red, which symbolises good fortune and joy. It is used with this year's ubiquitous design element: dog. According to the Chinese zodiac calendar, 2018 was the Year of Dog. Christian Dior also released a dedicated video to introduce the exclusive "Rose des vents" jewellery collection. Louis Vuitton created a cartoon dog based on the Japanese Shiba Inu breed for this Lunar New Year.

On the Bharat side, Diwali has been the most sought-after festival for these brands. A good example is a Spanish brand dedicated since 1953 to the creation of art porcelain figurines, Llardo. They came up with Lakshmi figurines and diyas made of porcelain for Diwali. Hermes had launched its saree for the Indian market, which had takers, but did not encourage the French luxury brand to come up with more. Jimmy Choo, too, has some collections dedicated to the Indian market. But they are destined for failure if they do not go deeper into understanding the traditions they are customising their collections for. For example, while both Diwali and Dhanteras are occasions for splurging and showcasing wealth, in the former, the buying is for gifting while in the latter, it is for within the family – preserving Lakshmi within the household. So, the customisations will be very different if a luxury brand chooses to tap into these markets.

While luxury brands have taken a step towards acknowledging the importance of these markets, they are yet to acknowledge the criticality of greater understanding of the traditions and its ethos. Understanding the customers and what they intend to showcase via the various days of celebrations of the wedding is the key to the multi-billion-dollar Indian wedding industry. These brands need to take a closer look at the various rituals and then they will understand the customers' needs that they are not able to meet or satisfy currently – basically the need gap. Customer immersion is the only way by which they will be able to strategize and thus understand the range of products that they can come up with to be an integral part of the celebrations. Indianisation of international luxury brands is the only way they can get a pie of the wedding market.

There is, however, a catch. These international brands need to also keep in mind that the right mix is the only solution to success. In their zeal towards becoming Indian, they can't lose their essence, which is the raison d'être.

So, the right portion to the multi-billion-dollar magical potion is the magical mantra to be invited in the big, fat Indian wedding.

CHAPTER 10

Trick of making luxe worth your wait

We are such stuff
As dreams are made on; and our little life
Is rounded with a sleep.

> William Shakespeare in *The Tempest*, Act 4, Scene 1

The immortal words by the bard capture the objective of any luxury brand. Luxury dazzles and weaving dreams with a touch of fantasy is what keeps the dazzle alive, ensuring the survival of a luxury brand.

The strategic aim of any luxury brand is to create aspirations. A neat trick that all the luxury brands play to keep the dreams going is that the product that they advertise the most is never available at their boutiques. Across the globe, they will make you wait while they keep fuelling your desire to own it by advertising it more and more.

A recent case is about Rolex GMT Master II, popularly known as 'Pepsi' because of its colour combination. This model was made popular by an American actor James Todd Spader in a series called Blacklist. After the official launch, the demand started to soar across all stores. So instead of producing more, Rolex decided that it will just keep increasing the waitlist. Two months back, I checked in Dubai Mall that the waiting time was four years. Hermes Birkin has been well known for an even longer waiting period. These brands believe the longer the waiting, the more the longing. The downside of it is that these brands also end up losing customers to competition because of unrealistic waiting periods.

These are the stuff dreams are made of, and so, when you actually have it, the dream is over. It is funny the way our minds work, especially of the Richie Rich (RR).

Another challenge these brands face is because of a certain characteristic of the consumer – relativity. Luxury is relative. What dazzles you may not dazzle me and definitely may not dazzle a Maharaja or, in today's parlance, the RR.

So, while it is comparatively easy to weave a dream for me, it is challenging to do the same for an RR who can easily get anything that money can buy. How can you create this El Dorado? This is where customisation plays a key role. While I may be enamoured by the sheer presence of a Rolls Royce Phantom, the RR, who already owns a few, will be equally enamoured with a Rolls Royce which has his or her initials and not of the Rolls Royce carved by the company on the bonnet in the same font and style. We frequently see cases wherein these companies love to customise their cars for these special customers by covering them with diamonds and rubies.

And last but not the least, another very effective strategy that luxury brands use to keep the dreams alive is by creating the "limited edition" myth. Let's give you a sneak peek into the minds of the RR when it comes to buying luxury goods. The fact that they can buy anything that has a price tag, is a double-edged sword cutting both ways. One, they are happy to know that they are people with means and so can afford almost anything in the realm of luxury brands. Second, because they can afford it, they are unhappy as there is no fun in it, no dream, no aspiration. The myth of limited edition comes to the rescue here. So even if the RR can afford such a luxury item, the dream is woven by money not being the decisive factor in possessing the same. So, this makes the owner feel special, even compared with the other RRs as he or she is the proud owner of a limited edition.

The RR's mind works in strange ways and so the luxury brands have to keep innovating to keep the dreams alive and their cash registers ringing.

CHAPTER 11

Images luxe conjures

What is the first thing that strikes you when you look at a luxury brand? What is the image a brand conjures in your mind? Is it a positive sentiment or negative? Is it inspiring or is it shameful? Does it make you long for it, make you yearn? Or it brings back a memory of a crime or scandal? For example, when you look at diamonds, do they bring thoughts of blood diamonds? Do you take an extra initiative to make sure the diamonds you are using are not bloody? This is where brand identity comes in.

When you come to know that the diamond is from De Beers or a Tiffany's, do you still have a doubt on its credibility? No, because these brands over the years have been able to establish their identity with clean diamonds. What the customer associates a brand's identity with makes all the difference. That perception alone can make or break a brand, and it becomes an integral part of the brand identity. Not only are you confident that these brands do not use blood diamonds, but you are also okay with paying a hefty premium for them. But do you have a mechanism by which you can be certain? No. However, it never matters as the perception war is already won.

Brand positioning is the key element when it comes to building perception in luxury. "The basic approach of positioning is not to create something new and different, but to manipulate what's already in the mind, to retie the connections that already exist," said Al Ries and Jack Trout in their book *Positioning: The battle for your mind.* Thus, it is all about how you are perceived in the eyes of the consumers and the art of manipulating that.

The idea of luxe is to dazzle and that dazzle essentially is perception. To me, a Rolls Royce Phantom exudes royalty and class. As I wrote in *Dark Luxe* on Phantom: "There is a saying that I run on reputation. I am the Phantom of reputation. I am the Rolls Royce Phantom. I am the mark of class, snobbery – the ultimate in luxury. When I drive down the road, people bow with respect and awe." However, to the Maharaja in that story, the same Rolls Royce Phantom was a mere collector of garbage. His perception is very different. The news that he has sent out a Phantom to collect garbage had spread like wildfire and had resulted in a steep fall in its sales in India. Just to put things in perspective, India market accounted for 25% global sales of Phantom in the 1920s. Perception made all the difference.

Let me give you another example. You see a socialite stepping out of a BMW carrying a Gucci clutch. You probably won't think that the clutch is a counterfeit. On the other hand, when another lady steps out of a radio taxi and is carrying the same clutch, a part in you screams that it has to be a fake. This is what perception is all about. The brand identity here is that if you are stepping out of a BMW, you are rich and affluent, and so can afford an expensive clutch. So, for Gucci, the brand identity is that it is expensive, so people who can afford expensive cars can easily afford expensive bags, but that can't be said of people who are travelling in a taxi.

The irony is that it is quite possible that in the first case, the clutch could be a fake, and in the second, a genuine one. The rich and the affluent often take resort to expensive first copies as they have to visit many parties every day and cannot afford to repeat their dress or stilettoes or clutch. Thus, first copies come to the rescue. And as they are aware of the popular perception, they know no one will doubt whether their clutch or stilettoes are genuine as long as they are stepping out of a BMW.

It is all a matter of creating the right identity by manipulating perception.

CHAPTER 12

Controversy, thy name is luxe

Let me first share the Met Gala controversy wherein two weeks before the Gala in 2023, the team behind the High Fashion Twitter Met Gala sent out a tweet that stated that they would not be holding their usual digital companion event to the annual Costume Institute Benefit, which is often referred to as fashion's biggest night, because their values do not align with the theme - Karl Lagerfeld.

While the fashion industry has long been critiqued for its lack of inclusivity, especially when it comes to larger bodies or race, Lagerfeld had no shame in deriding bodies, particularly women's bodies. Though he also struggled with his own body issues, going so far as to lose 92 lbs in a year, an experience he documented with a 2005 book titled The Karl Lagerfeld Diet, Lagerfeld frequently offered unsolicited critiques of other public figures like Adele, who he called "too fat," and Heidi Klum, "too heavy," while mocking movements like body positivity and making outrageous claims that anorexia was not as dangerous as junk food and TV and or that fashion is "the healthiest motivation for losing weight."

Let's rewind a little. Let us understand the Chinese luxury consumers and market, which came into the news for boycotting Italian luxury brand Dolce & Gabbana (D&G) over alleged racist remarks.

According to a recent study, by 2025, the value of the global luxury goods market will climb to around USD450 billion and 7.6 million Chinese households will represent USD150 billion of that pie, an amount equivalent to the combined size of the

US, the UK, French, Italian and Japanese markets in 2016. Chinese consumers will account for 44% of the total global market by 2025.

It is natural that all the luxury giants have their eyes on China. They have all started customising collections based on important events such as the Chinese New Year to showcase how important China is for them.

For Dolce & Gabbana too, the "Shanghai Great Show" was a step in that direction, in line with their strategy to capture this pie. But alas, it backfired. This Italian fashion house had to cancel this major show after controversial videos and offensive private Instagram messages, allegedly sent by co-founder Stefano Gabbana, went viral on social media. Celebrities and models in China deserted the brand immediately. The designer has, however, denied writing the messages, stating his Instagram account was hacked.

It all began with a promotional video featuring an Asian model in a red D&G dress, trying to use chopsticks to eat pizza, spaghetti and a giant version of the Italian pastry cannoli. A series of direct messages on Instagram went viral where Gabbana complains about criticisms of the video. The Italian designer is then accused of making derogatory remarks directed towards China and the Chinese people as he defends the ads. This resulted in a mass boycott in China, even after Gabbana's apology and a cry that his account was hacked.

Another example of such controversial remarks is by champagne brand Cristal. It was the delight of billionaire rapper Jay-Z and he had used it in his music videos, resulting in huge publicity. Unfortunately, the high was short-lived for the brand. *The Economist* interviewed Frederic Rouzaud, the then managing director of Cristal, in 2006 and he was asked how the owners felt about seeing rappers sip their gold in their music videos. "That's a good question," he replied, with a biting follow-up: "But what can we do? We can't forbid people from buying it. I'm sure Dom Perignon or Krug would be delighted to have their business." Jay-Z was appalled, and the brand suffered the brunt of their racist views.

Almost a decade ago, founder of another well-known fashion brand Tommy Hilfiger faced the storm when he allegedly said that doesn't want minorities wearing his clothes.

And then there is the controversial history of brands and their associations such as the story of Hugo Boss joining the Nazi party in 1931. The all-black SS uniform was produced by the Hugo Boss company, along with the brown SA shirts and the uniforms of the Hitler Youth. Some of his factory workers during this period were also French and Polish prisoners of war who were forced into labour.

These controversies have in almost all cases impacted the top-line and bottom-line of these luxury brands adversely and has also eroded the brand value to an extent that buyers decided not to be associated with them. These brands end up becoming a social stigma, an outcast in the respective impacted geographies among its hitherto-loyal clienteles. The need of the hour is a sensitisation drive among all luxury brands – from the owners to the ground attendants who directly handle customers every day. While these luxury majors clearly understand the economic importance of certain geographies such as China and Bharat, they fail to give any serious heed to their culture and history.

CHAPTER 13

Karl and the art of luxury brand legacy

The passing away of iconic fashion designer Karl Lagerfeld gave rise to a very important question – What will happen to his brand now? Which makes us think, how to create a brand legacy?

Lagerfeld, as Time magazine describes, the iconoclastic designer best known for being at the helm of Chanel for over three decades, as well as designing for Fendi and his own eponymous label, was famous for his innovative designs, his fantastical fashion shows, and his branding genius, both personally and professionally. He was one of the first designers to channel their creative leadership into becoming a public figure in their own right, cultivating the persona as "the Kaiser," an aloof sunglasses-wearing and ponytail sporting caricature of himself that catapulted him to almost as much attention as his designs for Chanel. Lagerfeld was also equally notorious for his sharp tongue and seeming lack of filter, both of which he deployed often and on many topics.

Will a customer still have the same unshakable faith in the brand when the icon is no longer running the show? When customers become loyal to a brand, especially a renowned one like Karl Lagerfeld, they do not buy it for the design or style or aesthetics or flaunt quotient alone. The personality of the icon becomes the X-factor, which demands the premium as well as the loyalty. So, when that icon is no longer there, the loyalty of the customers is bound to take a hit. In art, the creativity of the artist is captured on canvas and thus after the artist is gone, the prices soar. In fashion, once the icon is gone, there may be a sudden surge resulting from emotional buying by customers, but it is bound to fall soon.

Karl Lagerfeld was the creative director for two iconic brands – Chanel and Fendi. However, the dent these two fashion houses will suffer will be significantly less compared with the legendary designer's own fashion house. Chanel and Fendi, unlike his own brand, are no longer represented by faces or personalities.

Apple's situation after the death of Steve Jobs comes close to this issue that ails Lagerfeld's fashion house. While a lot of persona was attached to the products and Jobs was the face of Apple, the company was still able to move on after a brief setback, and one critical reason was the name – Apple, not Jobs.

Louis Vuitton did not face this danger when their creative designer Marc Jacobs moved on and started his own label. Gucci carried on successfully after Tom Ford left. But what if Tom Ford or Marc Jacobs decided to take a break from their own brands?

This leads to a Catch 22 situation. You can't gain complete trust of the customers without giving a face to the brand. On the other hand, if there's a prominent face to a brand, what happens when the face is not there anymore? What should be the right portion of persona that a brand creator needs to put in to leave a legacy?

Here are five golden rules:

1. The brand needs to create a perception that it is professionally run. This plays a key role in ensuring that while there is a face, the brand is run by professionals. Even after the death of Coco Chanel, the brand's legacy not only lived on, but also kept growing. The brand of Alexander McQueen, on the

other hand, faced a tough time after his untimely death. Apple, too, had a slight setback before it bounced back.

2. Faceless brands such as Rolex and Louis Vuitton thus have an edge. These brands are more affected by the demand cycles, not the presence or absence of personalities. These brands, however, have created a persona of their own, based on their style quotient. They have successfully used icons as brand ambassadors to give their brands a face, a persona and a legacy.

3. The billion-dollar questions for a brand creator are – when should he or she pour his or her personality into the brand and when should the brand start to develop its own persona? While establishing the brand should always be the primary responsibility, it is also important to give professionals a free hand to run the machinery. The creator should focus on the creative side of the business.

4. The key lies in succession planning. A brand creator needs to wake up to the thought of planning for a successor who will keep the legacy on. It is best if this successor gets some handholding from the creator so that he or she can imbibe the key elements of the brand personality, so that loyal customers do not feel cheated.

5. It is the brand promise that makes it powerful. The most important element for a brand to create a legacy is to keep its promises. This will help them create a history. *(Reference: The Luxe Inferno by author)*

CHAPTER 14

A fake, is a fake, is a fake

Why does a consumer spend hard-earned money, and that too willingly, on something that is not authentic? What can be the lure to buy a fake, a counterfeit? How can luxury brands make sensible people so blind that they make a beeline outside offline or online stores for getting their hands on these counterfeits?

Let me give you some salient pointers on luxury counterfeits:

- Growing at a breakneck speed of 40-45%, the luxury counterfeit market passed USD3 trillion-mark in 2023.

- There are grades of these luxury counterfeit products, and the best ones are called first copy. They are distinctly different from the so-called cheaper versions of fakes that are easily available online or offline.

- The two most counterfeited brands are Rolex and Louis Vuitton.

- Some e-commerce sites sell counterfeits declaring them as authentic, at unbelievable discounts. The photographs used in all such cases are illegally taken from the official websites of the luxury brand to create this myth of authenticity.

- It is estimated that 40% of sales of luxury counterfeit goods take place online. These digital accesses allow consumers to engage in counterfeiting trade anonymously and from any location. Even as distributors take efforts to shut down these sales, new ones appear as quickly as they are removed.

- There has been a surge in the growth of the counterfeit market with the onset of e-commerce. While earlier these fakes were bought secretly in blind alleys, now they can be shopped from your mobile and delivered at home, at your convenience.
- Data shows that 30% of consumers accidentally bought a fake product online over the last five years and 24% of consumers said they unwittingly purchased a counterfeit product in the last 12 months online.
- There are some distinct identifiers for all luxury brand goods that help sieve the fakes.

The growth of luxury sales over digital channels is tied to the shift in customer base to Millennials and Gen Z. Combined, these younger generations of affluent consumers will make up roughly 70% of the luxury market by 2025, contributing to 130% of luxury market growth.

Now let me delve a little deeper into this curious case of first copies. If you look at a fake Rolex Datejust or Day Date, there will be marked differences that even an untrained eye will be able to spot. But for a first copy, only expert eyes will be able to spot the differences. For example, a first copy watch will have high-quality steel, sapphire crystal case and precise mechanical movement like the original. The master watchmaker has not only replicated the complication with precision but also kept an eye on the identifiers. In my book *Dark Luxe*, I have shared the story of Master W who has been passing on this talent of fine watchmaking over generations. Now, unfortunately, he is compelled to make first copies, but he does it with the same dedication and pride.

For the past few years, in my quest for understanding luxe, I have been exploring and researching the counterfeit markets in Europe, Middle East, Southeast Asia and India. Speaking extensively to the sellers as well as buyers across these markets, I have gathered that there is a huge demand for luxury fakes, as they are cheap. Also, the demand for first copies is low across these markets as most consumers, according to these sellers, do not understand the difference and thus can't justify the price differential.

But why buy a fake? The blame falls squarely on the brand built by these luxury goods. They create an aspiration among the so-called 'have-nots' to own, rather possess these labels, these logos. It gives a sense of entitlement, most buyers said. And they assume that the people they are going to flaunt these labels to also will not be able to figure out whether it is a fake or authentic. Thus, the objective is to showcase, rather flaunt, to others one's entitlement and purchasing power. And thus, the rise and rise of the counterfeit market.

Counterfeits also give rise to democratization of luxury. Even the 'have-nots' can now flaunt the labels of the 'haves', albeit the counterfeits, that the former only could aspire for earlier. Even luxury brands are exploiting this sentiment with their masstige category.

What is curious about the first copy luxury product is that primary consumers are not the 'have-nots', but the 'haves'. This is a category which is a heavy consumer of luxury brands and prefers some first copies on the side. For example, a friend of mine told me that she has to go to three-four parties every night and she can't repeat the brands of her clutch or her stilettos. Thus, she has decided to mix and match originals and first copies, all for the eyes of the beholder. *(Reference: The Luxe Inferno by author)*

However, a fake is a fake is a fake!

CHAPTER 15

The Mythic Value of Luxury

Myths are an integral part of our lives. These stories have the power to transcend centuries, geographies and demographics. Myth is, however, interpreted in conflicting ways – collective dreams, outcome of an aesthetic play or a foundation of a ritual. Mythological figures are thus considered as personified abstractions, divinised heroes or decayed gods. Some claim that human societies merely express, through their mythology, fundamental feelings common to the whole of mankind, such as love, hate, revenge; they try providing explanations to phenomena which they cannot understand otherwise.

Let us look at myth from a philosophical perspective. There are indeed multitude of myths in Greek Philosopher Plato's dialogues: traditional myths, which he sometimes modifies, as well as myths that he invents, although many of these contain mythical elements from various traditions. He is both a myth teller and a myth maker. In general, he uses myth to inculcate in his less philosophical readers noble beliefs and/or teach them various philosophical matters that may be too difficult for them to follow if expounded in a blunt, philosophical discourse.

Coming back to more anthropological impact, moving from decayed gods and divinised heroes to more recognisable forms. For example, if evil claims prominence in a character, say depicted by grandmother, then it implies in such a society grandmothers are evil. Mythology reflects the social structure and the social relations. The purpose of mythology thus may be investigated, providing an outlet for repressed feelings.

Anthropologist Claude Levi Strauss says if there is a meaning to be found in mythology, this cannot reside in the isolated elements, which enter the composition of a myth, but only in the way those elements are combined. Although myth belongs to the same category as language, being, as a matter of fact, only part of it, language in myth unveils specific properties. Those properties are only to be found above the ordinary linguistic level; that is, they exhibit more complex features beside those to be found in any kind of linguistic expression.

In exhaustive studies of myth, and his book-length theoretical interventions on religious thought, Levi Strauss mined for what he called the "hidden harmonies" from a morass of random-seeming data sets. What transformed this arid-sounding undertaking into a fertile intellectual exercise was on one hand the raw material – the fantastic diversity of the ethnographic minutiae Lévi-Strauss obsessively ranged over; and on the other, the eclectic influences Lévi-Strauss brought to bear on this rich seam of material. [6]

Levi Strauss continues that in mythology, on one hand, anything is likely to happen. There is no logic, no continuity. Any characteristic can be attributed to any subject; every conceivable relation can be met. With myth, everything becomes possible. But on the other hand, this apparent arbitrariness is belied by the astounding similarity between myths collected in widely different regions. Therefore, the problem: if the content of a myth is contingent, how are we going to explain that throughout the world myths do resemble one another so much.

With this background on myth, let me explain this concept of mythic value. Myths are future-proof, small wonder that they are able to live for ages. But how are myths, with all the dimensions able to stand the test of time.

What makes myths live through ages is that they embody contradictions. Myths create a space in which two contradictions can co-exist. It is this co-existence that creates something that has a value that is timeless. This is called mythic value. Thus, the greater the contradiction, the higher will be the degree of the mythic value. It is this embodiment of contradictions that myths are so similar across varied cultures and geographies.

Let me first explain with a non-luxury example. Among all the creations of **Auguste Rodin**, the most famous is the bronze sculpture **"The Thinker" or "Le Penseur"**. The reason: it is the embodiment of the greatest contradictions of all times – Mind and Body.

The word luxury comes from the word luxe, which means "dazzle". What creates that dazzle? The core element of that dazzle is **that it represents something unique.** So, what keeps the luxury brand dazzling over the ages? The unique element that luxury brands that have stayed on for ages is mythic value. They have been an embodiment of contradictions passed on as a legacy of the heritage they were a part of.

The tales of luxury have a deep root in heritage and have always been a story of embodying contradictions. As stated earlier, the greater the contradiction, the greater the appeal of a luxury brand. The legend, the heritage continues to lure, continues to create awe, continues to remind the contradictions it represents – both simultaneously. That is why the heritage remains the greatest USP of any luxury brand even today. Thus, it is the mythic value stemming from the heritage that makes a brand iconic or legendary.

Let me explain with a few examples of how heritage plays a critical role in creating mythic value. The heritage is primarily originated from our Royalty.

Let's look at the case of the Maharaja of Patiala. An **Indian native Maharaja** adorning the most expensive **Cartier** crown necklace with the biggest **DeBeers diamond** that you can ever imagine. This would not have created such a legendary visual if the King were a Brit or European because here two contradictions meet — **East meets West**. Moreover, the popular perception is that of diamonds as a girl's best friend. But, a man's best friend? So, this imagery has in itself another contradiction – **Man and Diamonds**. This was the image of Maharaja of Patiala, who commissioned the largest order to the epitome of Western brand Cartier back in 1926. Now this B/W photograph is carefully showcased in all major Cartier showrooms, some of which I have visited, especially abroad. Cartier executives are trained to carefully mention the story to key clientele, to make the client buy into the "mythic value" of Cartier's luxury heritage. The client is made to feel one with the legacy of the brand that it carefully has chosen to showcase, as if the product is the conduit to the imagined community of royalty.

An **India native Maharaja** buying the epitome of reputation in Western culture – a **Rolls Royce**. And converting it into a garbage collector for the city. Had a European done this to an Indian brand, it would have been commonplace. Again, experience the visual appeal of East deconstructing West by embodying it. These visuals when analysed deeply show that they capture an embodiment of contradictions. These contradictions together create a mythic value in these brands that make them iconic. No wonder these legendary stories are alive for over a century and still able to generate awe.

If we look deeper into the case of the **Nizam** and his postmen, we will see the heritage and contradiction as well. If it were horses, it would not have been made through time. If is easy to connect horses with Indian Nizams, given the time and the heritage of royalty. But the moment horses are replaced with

Harley Davidsons. Heritage meets modernity creating mythic value.

Thus, it is the heritage that helps luxury brands identify and unlock the value of their myth – The Mythic Value of Luxury.

Luxe Book 2

About Luxe Book 2

The book is an essence of Prof Mahul Brahma's *Aesthetic Leadership in Luxury* and is a research-based manual for a CXO as well as an organisation to transform into an Aesthetic Leader. This book aims at understanding the origin and scope of aesthetic leadership and includes my lectures delivered in the United Kingdom. The book explores the uniqueness of businesses that are dependent on beauty, art, design and why these need unique leadership acumen wherein the leader himself or herself has to be an integral part of generating the competitive advantage – aesthetics. It also explores the strategic perspective of leading luxury brands with a certain finesse that only aesthetics can provide, especially while handling Quite Luxury with Aesthetes and Connoisseurs. It explains how an organisation needs to restructure itself towards creative- and aesthetic-centricity in luxury. The book explains the role of disruptors from technology space like Apple wherein design and aesthetic-obsessive behaviour is the core competency for charging super premium, behaving just like a luxury brand. The book is a comprehensive narration of the story of aesthetic leadership in luxury along the various strategy contours of art, beauty, design, creativity and of course, aesthetics. The book was launched in the UK in 2023.

Contents

Prologue: Aesthetic Leadership

Facets of Leadership

Lecture delivered in the United Kingdom: Quiet Luxury: Understanding Aesthetes and Connoisseurs

Lecture delivered in the United Kingdom: Communication Strategy for Aesthetic Leaders

Role of Visual Communication in Aesthetic Leadership

Role of Creativity in Aesthetic Leadership

Organizational Aesthetics in Luxury Brands

Exclusive Case Study: Aesthetic Leadership in Practice

A leader is best when people barely know he exists, when his work is done, his aim fulfilled, they will say: we did it ourselves.

Lao Tzu

Prologue: Aesthetic Leadership

The Greek word aisthesis refers to any kind of sensory experience regardless of whether it is sensuous or artistic. Philosopher Alexander Gottlieb Baumgarten is considered the father of aesthetics. Along with Vico (1744, reprinted in 1948), he contended that knowledge was as much about feelings as it was cognition (Baumgarten, 1750). Aesthetic knowledge involves sensuous perception in and through the body (Merleau-Ponty, 1962) and is inseparable from our direct experience of being in the world (Dewey, 1958; Gagliardi, 1996).

The contention that the felt meaning based on experience was just as important as cognitive understandings was made in contrast to Descartes' detached intellectual epistemology. Cartesian thinking did not so much separate the mind/body as simply ditch the body. As a result, the mind (cognitions, intellect, logic) was privileged as a source of knowledge and our sensory-based and embodied ways of knowing were marginalized. This marginalization is ironic because aesthetic experience shapes and precedes all other forms of knowledge (Husserl, 1960; Langer, 1942). *(Reference: Aesthetic Leadership by Hans Hansen, Arja Ropo & Erika Sauer)*

Let us first understand the raison d'etre of the term "aesthetic leadership". Aesthetics is defined as the philosophical study of beauty and taste. The term is closely related to the philosophy of art, which is concerned with the nature of art and the concepts in terms of which individual works of art are interpreted and evaluated. So, aesthetic leadership primarily concerns the manner in which artists, and other aesthetic workers, executes leadership within groups, communities and culture, often outside established positions of authority.

It is also quite possible that aesthetic leadership draws some of its power from the position of the aesthetic producer or rather creator, who is mostly outside conventional leadership positions. The leadership is rather centred around that key creator on whose aesthetic prowess the organisation is running.

Aesthetic leadership may not only refer to creativity or vision, rather it may emerge from insight into cultural, political, or interpersonal issues as well; aesthetic statements on social injustice or crucial cultural concerns; or, at a more general level, provide alternative ways of seeing problems, history or received wisdom. In this way, aesthetic leadership may either complement or contradict more traditional leadership forms, such as politics, religion, or management. It may be that aesthetic leadership draws some of its power from the position of the aesthetic producer outside conventional leadership positions.

Let me share a few examples are cited by academician Jonathan E. Schroeder in his writings: 1. Jacques-Louis David, whose famous painting The Death of Marat (1793) catalysed support for the French revolution by shrewdly mixing fine art with propaganda. During the eighteenth-century uprising, David reorganized the Académie, an important national institution – critical for authenticating and disseminating cultural and political opinions and trends – and he produced many spectacular propagandistic events, eventually being imprisoned for his political views.

2. Another iconic aesthetic leader, poet Czeslaw Milosz, drew attention to repression in Poland, and helped spark the Solidarity movement's success.

3. A final example concerns the Asian-American sculptor and architect Maya Lin, whose haunting Vietnam Veteran's memorial in Washington DC helped a nation – especially Vietnam veterans and their families – begin to come to terms with a tremendously debilitating and divisive epoch in American history. Lin, who, an undergraduate university student at the time, steadfastly refused to compromise her aesthetic principles during a bitter battle over her minimalist design, held to her strong, clear vision, as described in the Academy Award winning documentary of the rancorous debates about how the war should be memorialized (Mock 1995).

Behind every exquisite thing that existed, there was something tragic.

Oscar Wilde

Lecture delivered in the United Kingdom

Quiet Luxury: Understanding Aesthetes and Connoisseurs

Now luxury is a business where aesthetics plays a pivotal role. I will not look at luxury and managing luxury business with the lens of aesthetic leadership.

In Book 1, I have categorised luxury consumers. Among the four only two categories of luxury consumers are relevant to businesses that need aesthetic leadership:

Let's first meet the **Connoisseurs**. This genre is passionate in certain areas of interest and makes it a point to be well informed and knowledgeable about it. These categories could be art, scotch, wine, watches, writing instruments, cigars, horses, and others. These connoisseurs get together and appreciate the finer aspects of their passion. They look down upon people who do not share their passion. They form clubs and get together for a quiet appreciation of the luxury of creation. It may be a horology society or a wine club or a scotch club or a cigar group. Being rich is a necessary but certainly not a sufficient condition for being a part of this exclusive group of connoisseurs. You need to belong to a certain class to be a part of this group.

They will spend their time and money in pursuit of the collection of personal passion points. They make the pursuit of their area of passion a mission and pursue it with zest. When it comes to limited editions or handcrafted editions or spirit of the bygone era, these connoisseurs will not bat an eyelid for spending a fortune.

And then comes the **Aesthetes**. To this genre, the brand is much less important than the design. Aesthetes are luxury consumers purely because they have arrived at a state of income due to which they can indulge in their love for design among luxury brands or products. They will shell out a bomb because the object of desire is hand stitched and not because of the label. They pride themselves for having an eye that picks out the unique and bold in design. Again, money or the brazen display of affluence is frowned upon by this category of buyers. They are more into the appreciation of finer things of life, and money surely can't develop that faculty.

The difference between them and the connoisseur is that the latter has certain passions which they follow with zeal and the quality and craftsmanship are very important. However, for the former category, it is the aesthetic appeal, the look, the intricacies of the design that appeal to their senses. They are also likely to pursue this aesthetic across categories, unlike a connoisseur. *(Reference: Decoding Luxe by Mahul Brahma)*

In the universe of luxury, the rules of the game for luxury brands and houses are very different as the customer need is very unique. The two above categories are firm believers in something called "Quiet Luxury". These are the uber rich who are very subtle in their approach towards luxury. They will make sure that their flaunting is only understood by a select category of luxury consumers. These are the big-ticket consumers or rather patrons. Therefore, obsession with design and aesthetics is the only way a brand can generate loyal high-end customers. The toughest challenge is to keep alive a sense of aspiration for the brand. The entire organisation needs to be recast based on aesthetic prowess of the differentiator-creators.

The other two not-so-quiet categories are **Flaunters** and **Experientialists**. The latter spend on experiences. Luxury to them conjures images suspended in time and space, not having the press of daily life and work responsibilities thrusting into their minds as they enjoy the escape from the mundane. In their structured, predictable lives their find an escape in five-star hotel stays, fine dining, and adventure trips.

A genuine leader is not a searcher for consensus but a moulder of consensus.

Martin Luther King Jr.

Lecture delivered in the United Kingdom

Communication Strategy for Aesthetic Leaders

So let us now look into the communication strategy for Aesthetic leaders as well as for aesthetic organisations.

The organisation as a whole has one point agenda: to communicate to all stakeholders, especially external, that it is obsessed by aesthetics and design. The second point agenda is to showcase, more so internally, that its structure is primarily centred around the aesthetic prowess of the leader. To be a leader, you do not have an option of not being aesthetic.

The core communication that needs to be propagated across all media is that the organisation has zero tolerance in terms of aesthetic excellence.

The second agenda is to build the profile of the leader as one who is driven by aesthetics and design. There is a huge role of storytelling in this segment wherein stories of eccentric behaviour towards obsession for design and aesthetics need to do the rounds so that no one questions the leadership. The leader needs to also demonstrate a certain behavioural pattern that establishes him/her as the last word in aesthetics and design. This not only helps in establishing the trust of the patrons but also helps in keeping the organisational balance under check.

No matter how much unconventional it is to cite the example of a tech company in luxury business, I can't possibly explain this without citing the example of Steve Jobs and Apple. Steve Jobs created a mythic value for not only him but also for his company – a combination of two contradictions of aesthetics or design and technology. Apple's obsession with design has made it a leader and Jobs has communicated the obsession with design in every demonstration during the launches. He not only established his prowess as an aesthetic leader but also established the supremacy of Apple as an aesthetic leader in the industry.

Creative designers in various luxury or fashion houses are given a free hand to create a team aligned to the aesthetic needs of the company or brand to strengthen the competitive advantage. When they leave, there is a void in aesthetically leading the company or brand. Apple faced it after Jobs' demise, fashion houses like LVMH and Gucci keeps facing it when their creative heads move on and build their own labels, such as Marc Jacobs or Tom Ford.

Communication thus plays a strategic role in keeping together the reputation of the brand during that period of crisis so that aggressive branding via storytelling can keep the margins intact.

Communication strategy has to be completely aligned to the aesthetic leader's objectives of positioning the brand with storytelling being the biggest ammo. In aesthetic communication, stories open the pre-frontal cortex of the brains of the patrons, luring them to loosen their purses. The premium charged is all thanks to the aesthetic leadership of the brand and even the smallest crisis due to diversity or racial intolerance or gender-insensitivity in communication can give a fatal blow to the brand.

It is thus always walking a tightrope when majority of your clients are GenZ millionaires, who are sensitive and a believer in diversity, inclusion, gender-tolerance and sustainability!

The greatest leader is not necessarily the one who does the greatest things. He is the one that gets the people to do the greatest things.

Ronald Reagan

Facets of Leadership

There's always a shroud of mystery behind leadership. A kind of an X factor that somehow magically is able to align itself and solve the problem. Boal and Hooijberg in 2000 reaffirmed Pettigrew (1992), who stated that "We still know little about why and how top teams and other groupings look the way they do, the processes by which top teams go about their tasks, how CEOs engage with their immediate subordinates, and how, why, and when the upper echelons engage in fundamental processes of problem sensing, decision making, learning, and change". This observation suggests that deeper research is required to link strategic leadership at the individual and group levels.

The responsibilities of strategic leaders to lead others in dynamic environments are particularly informed by micro-level theories incorporating situational aspects. For example, the basic assumption of contingency theories of leadership is that no leadership style is best in all situations, and that the leader's ability to lead followers is contingent upon factors such as the leader's preferred style, the capabilities and behaviours of followers, and the resources, support, and coordination available. Nevertheless, the scope of theories including Fiedler's (1967) contingency model of leadership, House's (1971) path-goal theory, and Leader Member Exchange (LMX) theory (Graen & Uhl-Bien, 1995) has generally focused on the characteristics of the work environment, not the external environment. *(Reference: Transcendent leadership: Strategic leadership in dynamic environments by Prof Len Nanjad)*

The elements of authentic leadership proposed by Luthans and Avolio are subsumed by the character strengths presented by Peterson and Seligman. Although the character strengths were not intended strictly as elements of leadership, we could not identify any element that was not directly related to leadership of self. Peterson & Seligman (2004, p. 28) identify "six core moral virtues that emerge consensually across cultures and throughout time."

Individuals will have personal dispositions and face contextual factors that affect their ability to fulfil their responsibilities at the three levels. Some strategic leaders have risen to the top because of their capacity to lead others but may not be well equipped for leadership of the organization; other leaders may be parachuted into situations where they are expected to make strategic changes but lack the ability to lead others. In this section, we look at different scenarios of strategic leadership and their implications in terms of firm performance, according to Nanjad.

Let me share the three levels of leadership towards self, others and organisational, as defined by Prof Nanjad in his paper:

Level 1: If a strategic leader's sole focus is leadership of others with limited attention to the self and the organization, firm performance will also suffer. In this case, followers identify with the leader and have high levels of motivation, commitment, and loyalty.

Level 2: Additionally, today's turbulent contexts tend to allow CEOs only short tenure at the top, so strategic leaders who do not attend to the self may lack "staying power." A strategic leader with a high level of leadership of others and organization and low leadership of self will be associated with high firm performance; this performance will, however, be lower than that of firms with strategic leaders excelling at the three levels of leadership.

Level 3: The transcendent leader, who has high levels of leadership of self, others, and organization, will be associated with the highest level of firm performance

Sometimes, the follower becomes a leader because a leader is not a specific person, it is any person performing the role of a leader. Leaders (the persons performing the role of leadership) are dispensable but not the role of a leader or leadership (Choi & Schnurr, 2014). For example, in self-directed teams, there is no designated leader but there is leadership; the team has to have direction, the team has to be equipped and inspired, monitored, evaluated and eventually it has met its objectives (Hill, 2016).

In Rethinking Leadership Theories, Prof Emmanuel Mango has made an effort towards consolidating 66 theories that govern leadership. It is found out that leadership is built on six foundational domains – character, characteristics, people practices, institutional practices, context and outcomes (CCPICO). These six domains resulted in an integrative leadership model, according to Prof Mango, which is ethical and effective leadership (EEL).

Despite the vital role played by leadership across different spheres of the society, numerous scholars argue that extant leadership development literature is shallow on leadership development theories (Snook et al., 2012; Day, Fleenor, Atwater, Sturm, & Mckee, 2014; Volz-Peacock, Carson & Marquardt, 2016). It is Prof Mango's understanding that leadership development is learning what leadership is and how to lead, particularly how to be an ethical and effective leader.

Another interesting perspective is 'authentic leadership'. The majority of work in this area, however, remains at the theory development stage, with less than a handful of studies to date being of an empirical nature. Furthermore, the concept has not been examined specifically from the upper echelon's perspective, but rather treated similarly to many other theories of leadership, as operating at any level within the organization where one directs the activities of group (Yukl, 1998). It is our intent herein to explore authentic leadership at the top of the organization and how the cognitive bases of the authentic strategic leader are reflected in organizational outcomes such as an organizational culture supportive of learning (Hambrick & Mason, 1984). *(Reference: The Art of Conversation: How Authentic Leaders Influence Organisational Learning by Prof Daina Mazutis and Prof Natalie Slawinski)*

The authors add that authentic strategic leaders must also be willing to self-declare, or to communicate learnings about themselves with others in the organization, otherwise followers will remain unaware about a leader's core values and beliefs (Goffee & Jones, 2006). Extending this logic, they said leaders who exhibit a heightened ability to understand their internal self-schemas will also be able to better detect their personal biases (increased self-awareness) and, if coupled with the ability to communicate these biases, will be more likely to be able to correct for these biases within the conversations that they are engaging in at all levels in the organization. Furthermore, authentic leaders at the top of the organization will also implement diagnostic systems, rules and procedures that institutionalize self-awareness as a key component of formal feedback mechanisms, helping individuals learn about themselves (Berson et al., 2006), thereby encouraging a culture of authentic dialogue throughout the organization.

Another core area is of leadership is empathy. In my column for Reputation Today magazine I have elaborated on the same.

Let us first clarify the difference between sympathy and empathy as this difference means a world in the realm of media communication, especially leadership communication. According to Oxford Advanced Learner's Dictionary the difference is between feeling sorry for someone and the ability to understand and person's feeling or experience. The nuance is critical because in the latter case there is action involved, especially through communication.

As an MD or CEO, one needs to take action, every moment. Taking tough calls are an integral part of job description. And a leader needs to do it very effectively, making sure that every such action is either preceded or followed by transparent empathetic communication showing that the leader understands and cares. For leaders, it needs a little recalibration of their minds, just feeling bad or sympathetic is not good enough.

For example, if an organisation has to take a business decision of rightsizing workforce to keep it viable then empathy in leadership communication becomes critical. The tone and tenor of the communication to the stakeholders is the cornerstone of a leadership communication.

It is not only enough to be empathetic, but also important to communicate as well. Every stakeholder needs to be communicated the rationale behind any tough decision as above. Some leaders choose to be silent during such period of transition, this is bad leadership. Every key decision needs to be communicated by the leader and the tenor should have empathy. The leader should not come across as somebody who does not care or lacks a heart. The demonstration of strength and resilience of a leader lies in being empathetic and kind under duress. Communication thus needs to clearly define the premise that includes how the leader is with the stakeholders and not someone who is cold and refuses to understand the distress scenario.

Design is a funny word. Some people think design means how it looks. But of course, if you dig deeper, it's really how it works.

Steve Jobs

Role of Visual Communication in Aesthetic Leadership

Visual Communication comprises two elements communication design and graphic design. While communication design refers to crafting a message that educates, motivates, and engages the viewer, graphic design uses design principles to communicate that message in a way that is clear and eye-catching to the intended audience.

What visual communication is really about at its core is selecting the elements that will create the most meaning for your audience. These elements usually include text, icons, shapes, imagery, and data visualizations.

Jacques Bertin (1983) explored design principles in data visualization and cartography, and the statistician Edward Tufte (2001) developed theory within data visualization and information design. The challenge for visual communication design was that little research had come from a visual communication design perspective, been researched within its parameters, or adopted by its practitioners. The contribution of visual perception research on visual communication design is still somewhat uncertain, yet the field of visual communication design would benefit by knowing how perception theories can be used for design research and which ones inform the process of design creation.

The initial findings by Prof Lorenzo Imbesi indicate that design effectiveness can be measured, but to use the measurement criteria and tools, it requires that the researcher, or designer, understands the theories behind them. It is, therefore, necessary to build awareness within the community of visual communication design educators, practitioners and other communication professionals, of these findings, and to develop more interdisciplinary research that can inform the discipline of visual communication design, and subsequently, lead to the development of a comprehensive design, and design research, toolkit.

Given that the average attention span has been reduced to eight seconds, or less, visual communication has started playing a key role in leadership.

So, the idea is to communicate leadership messaging with pictures, images, graphics, charts, graphs, infographics, and visual reports. Thus, making semiotics play a critical role in strategic decision making.

So, when it comes to the fields of art and luxury where aesthetics and design are critical, there is a need for the leader to be an expert visual communicator of the essence of the organisational trajectory. So not only being aesthetically strong but also being able to visually communicate the criticality of aesthetics as a part of organisational DNA becomes a key characteristic of an aesthetic leader.

In the business of luxury, aesthetics is the USP that gives it a niche so that a premium can be charged to the buyers of quiet luxury - Connoisseurs and Aesthetes.

So verbal communication has to take a back seat as the game is to dazzle…a game of luxe. So visual communication becomes the key when the key objective of the organisation is to manufacture aspiration. So visual communication plays a key role in whetting the appetite of key luxury clients as well as inspiring the team to keep striving for excellence in design and aesthetics.

Birth of an advertisement: A photograph of an exquisite diamond necklace versus a description of the same in 2-3 lines. Even the most profound thousand words will not be able to create the impact of that one visual. The necklace, the neck that adorns it…and the afterglow of the face. A true customer delight in one picture. This is the power of visual communication.

Cross-cultural and cross-traditional reach: The beauty of visuals is that it has the capability to cut across cultures and traditions, even demographics.

Every great design begins with an even better story.

Lorinda Mamo

Role of Creativity in Aesthetic Leadership

Creativity is a pivotal quality when it comes to luxury business, or for that matter any business. However, if we look at the existing organisational hierarchical system, we will find the most creative person will be in the lowest rung of the system. As you go up the ladder you will find people who are more system-oriented and structured, focused on keeping the machinery well-oiled. Any idea that comes from the lowest run of professionals who are new to the system are well-appreciated but seldom applied. Therefore, the creative mind feels a sense of isolation and dejection. This system is a creativity killer.

However, corporations survive such a system because of their nature. Their USP can be carved out based on price-competitiveness, liaisons, ecosystem manipulations, among other things. While one can always argue that such differentiators can be created better if creativity can find some breathing space in the existing system, it seldom happens. The reality remains that a pseudo-creative system is created which acts as a veil to cover the real story of being comfortable with the known and fearing the unknown.

The only well-known exception is Apple. In spite of being a tech company, creativity and design, aesthetics as well as in technology is held supreme. So, the organisation was developed by Steve Jobs to make creativity and innovation the bedrock.

In luxury business, however, creativity has to take centre stage. The USPs create the premium. So, the most creative person, even if the junior-most, once identified, will be elevated to the topmost creative position, if he/she so deserves. Once there is proof of the idea, there is no looking back. It is the need of the business.

Therefore, organisationally there has to be a flexibility so as to accommodate the best of creative ideas and thus the power-centricity has to be defined according to creative prowess.

Make it simple, but significant.

Don Draper

Organisational Aesthetics in Luxury Brands

Organizational theorist Chester Barnard (1938) said management was "aesthetic rather than logical" and better described by terms such as "feeling, judgment, and sense," but organizational studies has taken a scientific realist approach in search of effectiveness. Ottensmeyer (1996) pointed out that though we consistently experience and refer to organizations in aesthetic terms, we have not approached them that way academically.

In organisations such as LVMH, Gucci or any other luxury or fashion conglomerate wherein "the aesthetic factor" determines premium of the brand...being aesthetic-focused is a strategic objective. Therefore, every organisational strategy, including organogram has to be aligned to pay their respects to the masters of aesthetics.

So while it is art and beauty, it is also a multi-billion-dollar business. Aesthetics gives the competitive advantage to the organisation that aims to thrive in the luxe conundrum.

It is always that one creative genius who designs the clutter breaker, taking the brand to its summit. The entire organogram becomes dependent on how to provide the right manpower as well as ecosystem for this genius to keep doling out the competitive advantage that is killing the competition and enabling the organisation to charge a premium that is near-absurd.

Organisational aesthetics is not only about being aesthetic, it is mostly about sensing the aesthetics that the market will pay a premium for, a consumer behaviour that changes every season, sometimes overnight.

These market moving aesthetic bosses actually tell the clients what to flaunt and what to throw away. Reminds me of something another aesthetic used to say about his products: "Our job is to figure out what they're going to want before they do". Yes, you guessed right it was Steve Jobs. Besides the technological prowess, Apple has essentially been an aesthetic organisation. Design was God, pouring the blessings both revenue-wise as well as appreciation-wise. A cut above the rest.

This is the beauty of Apple, wherein it has made an entry even when I was talking of LVMH and Gucci.

Strati (1992, 1996, 1999) is responsible for introducing an aesthetic approach to organizational studies. Aesthetics provides a philosophical point to develop an alternative to the mainstream paradigm that emphasized the logical, rational, and linear nature of organizational practices such as management and leadership (Ropo, Parviainen & Koivunen, 2002). Since then, the empirical and theoretical analysis of the relations between aesthetics and organization has been well-established. Several reviews are present of the organizational literature on aesthetics and various codifications of the field of organizational aesthetics (Dean, Ottensmeyer, & Ramirez, 1997; Gagliardi, 1996; Ramírez, 2005; Strati, 1999; Taylor & Hansen, 2005).

An interesting perspective by Dobson (1999), wherein an aesthetic organisation classifies managers as technicians, moral managers, and aesthetic managers. The emergence of the aesthetic management paradigm places the aesthetic manager as an artisan in an aesthetic firm, seeking excellence in craft instead of an exclusive pursuit of profit. Similarly, Dickinson & Svensen (2000) outline what will constitute a beautiful corporation in the coming aesthetic age. At the managerial level, Austin & Devin (2003) contrast artful making with industrial making in comparing artful managers to theatre directors. Guillet De Monthoux, Gustafsson, & Sjostrand (2007) provide an array of cases that explores aesthetic leadership in different contexts. *(Reference: Aesthetic Leadership by Hans Hansen, Arja Ropo & Erika Sauer)*

Design is intelligence made visible.

Alina Wheeler

Exclusive Case Study: Aesthetic Leadership in Practice

In this chapter we will exclusively look into an Indian luxury brand that has been practicing aesthetic leadership for a very long time, may be even before the term was coined, like most traditional luxury brands globally. I interviewed the two young Managing Directors Dr Ketan Chokshi and Mr Jatin Chokshi of Narayan Jewellers, who themselves are ace jewellery designers, to take a deeper look into how they practice aesthetic leadership. Narayan Jewellers in a modernist traditionale luxury designer brand, creating a mythic value by embodying a heritage of almost a century with an ultra-modern essence.

1. In luxury space how significant is luxury and design?

Well, design is one of the most important elements to build luxury as luxury comprises highest aesthetic (design and innovation), finest quality, rarity-exclusivity, limited availability, and embodiment of contradictions.

At Narayan, the mission statement is "to deliver jewellery masterpieces which are designed with innovation, rarity of raw material, engineered technically with very high aesthetic (design) value."

2. What are the 5 key attributes of an aesthetic leader?

- Understanding of organisational aesthetics
- Moral purpose

- Emotional intelligence
- Empathy
- Sensitivity

3. How was aesthetic leadership managed historically in NJ as it is almost a century old?

For any aesthetic leadership, design and quality need to be the first principles. At Narayan Jewellers it is no different. My grandfather established this retail company in the year 1940 in Vadodara with a capital of 51 rupees. In this industry we are sixth generation and about 140 years old.

There are two things which my grandfather and my father always said were "there is a very thin or hair line difference between passion and greed" (which is *Dhagas* and *Havas* in Hindi and Gujarati) and "be true to yourself" (*Apne se kabhi jhooth mat bolna*).

Therefore, whenever they took decisions on things like…

- Design
- Quality
- Pricing
- Transparency
- Customer service
- Social responsibility

…They always followed these principles and maintained the spectacular aesthetic leadership very gracefully with all stakeholders and channel partners.

4. Challenges of an organisation that runs on dominance of aesthetics. Both of you, at a very early age, have taken over the reins of NJ. How did

you establish your leadership in NJ because unlike other organisations it has to be earned in an aesthetic leadership environment?

Well, me and Jatin inherited a 70-year-old young baby 12 years ago. By this time, we were already in business with our father for nearly 15 years and therefore we were well versed with most of the leadership principles. The toughest thing was the independent decision making now as a captain of ship.

We have always kept both the guiding principles of our predecessors as our lodestone. We added our emotional intelligence and with the help of new age digital solutions of more defined system, structure, process, policy, roles and responsibilities and transparency, we could very well earn not only the same but also more love and respect and trust from patrons and 360-degree stakeholders, both internal and external.

5. As aesthetic leaders you have to restructure the entire organisation based on aesthetic dominance, stating the supremacy of design over other attributes. What challenges did you face and what opportunities did you create?

Having a strong DNA of design, backed by our expert academia, we have graciously enhanced the aesthetic dominance of design over other attributes. The biggest challenge or rather the inherent challenge when you are much ahead of time is to constantly have the right team members in various roles and responsibilities in our company. All other factors can be made constant, but this is the most variable challenge in an aesthetically-driven organisation. Designing the organisation based on aesthetic prowess and keeping the key people in that system are the most challenging task of all.

To overcome this, we keep constantly growing the supremacy of aesthetics and design and thereby keep the stakeholders focused on design and aesthetic-driven performance.

It is our prowess in aesthetics and design that we have received international recognitions such as:

- Only brand from India to be a part of, for eight consecutive years, Forevermark Red Carpet collection for Oscars
- Only brand to be showcasing at the New York Fashion Week for nearly eight seasons
- Participation at prestigious auctions of Sotheby's and Christies

We gracefully say we are Modernist Traditionale Luxury Designer Brand with exclusive one-in-a-million designs!

Luxe Book 3

About Luxe Book 3

The book is an essence of Prof Mahul Brahma's *Luxe Inferno*, which is a philosophical quest for the true meaning of luxe. It traces the journey of a luxe-o-holic through the nine circles of Inferno described by Dante Alighieri in Divine Comedy. It is a heady mix of facts and fiction comprising in-depth analysis of the various facets of luxury, based on research spanning over decades.

Contents

Prologue

Luxe is all about perceptions

Part A

Luxe Inferno

1. Love at first sight
2. The power
3. The new identity
4. The clash
5. To hell and back
6. The Paradiso

Part B

Perception

1. Musings of millennial millionaires
2. Masstige – Luxury of the Masses
3. Of Flaunters and Bling Economy
4. The art of subliminal marketing
5. Darkness behind the veil of luxury
6. Of aspirations and mind games
7. Discovering facets of luxe identity
8. The luxe legacy
9. Philosophy behind Branding Desire

Part C Epilogue

Prologue

Luxe is all about perceptions

The fun fact about luxe is that if it looks expensive, it surely is.

The luxury industry runs on creating perceptions, one after the other, where each one tries to topple another. Brand custodians all over the world have sleepless nights in creating these perceptions and then creating some more. It is the primary preoccupation of the dream merchants in the luxury industry. It is the perception that justifies the steep premium paid by price-sensitive Indian customers.

Branding luxe is all about conjuring beautiful and fanciful images in the minds of the customers. And so, every luxury brand prefers to conjure some magic – a perception. "Most expensive" as a tag that customers drool over, is certainly not easy to get. The natural corollary to this tag is - why is it so expensive? It won't matter if you just keep hiking your price; there has to be a demand created for it. Perception is the key element is creating this demand. So let me take you through three key strategic perception-enablers that luxury brands have been exploiting since the beginning of time and will surely keep exploiting till the end of time.

Razzle Dazzle: Remember that news of Azzam, the largest yacht in the world, or the diamond and ruby-studded 24-carat gold bodied Rolls Royce Phantom, or the most expensive wine Domaine de la Romanée-Conti or DRC ($551,314), or the most expensive bottled water Beverly Hills 90H20 Luxy Collection Diamond Edition ($100,000 per bottle), or Saluki, the most expensive dog ($5,000). These are the stuff that dreams are made of, and they create the "world's most expensive" perceptions. This razzle-dazzle is the quickest and easiest means of creating a perception to conjure dreams that make spending millions and billions sound so justified.

Rarity: This is a very potent key to creating perception that can make people loosen their purse strings. The perception of rarity can be classified into two categories:

i) Ancient artefacts made by artisans who are no longer alive, paintings or sculptures by greats like Leonardo Da Vinci or Michelangelo, or an object, say a writing instrument or a watch used by a famous personality who is no longer alive (like Napolean Bonaparte or Mahatma Gandhi). Take for instance the priceless death mask of King Tut. These artefacts, paintings or writing instruments or watches were not rare when these well-known figures were alive; they never fetched billions at Sotheby's. Most of the great artists such as Vincent van Gogh died penniless while now their art is fetching billions of dollars. Blame it on the perception of rarity!

ii) When a watchman tries to create a complicated mechanism like a tourbillon that will give precision to a mechanical watch, this is rarity. Every such rare watch, such rare mechanical movement is painstakingly crafted by masters over months and may be years. Such pieces are rare. This is same for any artefact or a piece of art. The man hours put into its creation give the perception of rarity to these objects.

Exclusivity: Every individual longs to be special and not ordinary. They want to receive special treatment; they want to be looked up to and envied. They desire to be emulated, they desire to belong to a certain club of exclusivity, where entry in by invitation only. Luxury brands like Rolex and Louis Vuitton rely heavily on this enabler. If you own a Rolex, you will "live for greatness" and be an integral of an exclusive notional club of all owners of Rolex, such as President John F Kennedy or Martin Luther King Junior, or even tennis star

Roger Federer. Or Louis Vuitton telling you if you own their trunks or duffle bags, then you will know that "there are journeys that turn into legends", which a famous ad campaign featuring "Core values" of the LV brand with Sir Sean Connery, Bono, Francis Ford Coppola and Angelina Jolie. This is selling the perception of rising beyond the ordinary, becoming exclusive.

Part A
Luxe Inferno

'All hope abandon, ye who enter here'

CHAPTER 1

Love at first sight

If you are a business journalist, very soon in the profession, you develop an immunity towards large financial numbers. So much so that you develop an apathy towards figures which are less than nine or ten zeroes. The rationale being that, these figures, do not make headlines. This attitude gives clarity in terms of how not to be awed by multiple zeroes. When you report or edit, you do that without any awe or disdain.

It was after a few years of hard-core business journalism that our protagonist, D, or let's say, 'Dante', got an opportunity to explore the feature side of business. A newspaper was launched which decided to bring out a magazine on luxury brands. The Editor-in-Chief, V, or, let's say 'Virgil', told Dante it will be a great opportunity for him to explore this wonderful world of luxury.

Virgil had been a feature writer all his life and thus had limited understanding of hard-core news. Dante, on the other hand, was a hard-core news person and was not convinced that he would enjoy the so-called 'lighter side of business journalism'. But Virgil was determined and started narrating stories of his adventures in covering features and how it was a great learning experience. What Dante thought he would miss the most was the adrenaline rush that came with hard news. Dante liked Virgil's style, his love for finer things of life and his love for branded luxury. From his training as a hard-core journalist, he thought Virgil's flaunting of luxury brands was quite shallow. However, at some level, Dante too, felt good about the finer things of life.

Dante agreed to take on the job, but couldn't help but ask Virgil, "Why me? I am a very blunt instrument. Getting news from tough cookies comes more easily to me than appreciating fine craftsmanship."

Virgil smiled and said, "Welcome to the world of luxury."

Dante quickly retorted, "The world of luxe."

Virgil said, "Lux? The soap?"

Dante replied, "Luxe with an 'e'. This means 'dazzle' and is the origin of the word 'luxury'. You see, there are a few advantages of being a good quizzer."

The days ahead of a newspaper launch are like a roller coaster ride, high on adrenaline. No fixed timings, no office norms, no punching in or out. You come in at your own time and leave whenever you feel like. Or stay back. It is a cycle of intense planning and then execution, only to be dismantled the next moment. Just like a Jacques Derrida's 'Theory of Deconstruction', life goes on destroying and creating, in a rhythm. Dante's challenge was to understand luxury in the midst of this chaos. He started researching on the subject and very soon realized that there was no literature on luxe or luxury. All the writings had been mere product reviews with "price of request" tags and high-resolution pictures. That is all. Dante was in a spot. He was too proud to ask Virgil for a way out as he had taken it up as a personal challenge.

It was his day off and Dante decided to pay a visit to the newly-opened luxury mall in town. He was not one to give in to shopping, so mall visits were rare. Not a fan. Days off were few and far between, with the deadline pressure of the launch, but even the rare ones were spent mostly reading.

This trip was purely for academic purpose. To get a feel of luxe. The mall was a little different from the usual ones. Quite decently designed, and the best thing was, quite dignified and not in your face, like the others in the city.

Dante had decided that the first day will be for observation; some window shopping to get a feel of the luxury brands, the visual merchandise, but most importantly, to watch the buyers – and their reaction to luxe!

The first was a Louis Vuitton boutique. He first spotted a beautiful trunk which was on display. The design of the truck was beautiful, the stitches were exquisite, and the vintage touch had a very alluring feel. He could not stop himself and went near it. He started to closely observe the trunk, which was genuinely old and was like a fine piece of art. He thought he was in a gallery, appreciating a classic. As an artist, how could he not appreciate art? And what was in front of him was pure art! The boutique manager walked up to him, smiled and said, "In 1928, the Maharaja of Jammu & Kashmir placed orders for custom-made thirty trunks with us. This one was recently donated to us by the family. LV had customized it for the Maharaja. Talking of LV trunks, let me share some more interesting facets of this long and loving courtship of LV with Indian Royalty. Sir, Louis Vuitton was unique in use of valuable materials and precious leathers. The luxury house was always able to serve special requests from the Indian Maharajas, no matter how extraordinary, elaborate or detailed the demands were. A certain Maharaja had ordered all the trunks imaginable for the most diverse of items – golf clubs, turbans, decorations, polo sticks, horseshoes, colonial helmets, among others."

Dante didn't realize how time went by; he was completely engrossed by Karthik's story. Dante smiled and introduced himself as a journalist who wrote on luxury. Karthik seemed happy with the introduction and offered him tea and continued with his story. Dante spent the next forty-five minutes in the boutique.

It was love at first sight.

Karthik ushered him to the door and asked him to visit again. In this whole story telling session, things happened like magic. Dante just fell in love with the brand, the story, the legacy and desperately wanted to be a part of it. Small wonder, he swiped his card and left the store with an LV monogrammed, hand-stitched sling. Stories can be addictive.

It was Dante's first luxury purchase. He was elated. He now owned a bit of luxe. He visited the Cartier boutique next, while observing the old photographs adorning the Trinity necklaces, the manager Azam walked up to him and noticing the keen interest, decided to share a story. Sir, in 1926, the Maharaja of Patiala commissioned us, Cartier, our largest till date, to remodel his crown jewels, which included the 234.69 carat De Beers diamond. The result was a breath-taking Patiala necklace weighing 962.25 carats with 2,930 diamonds. He pointed towards the picture of the Maharaja adorning the crown necklace. Dante introduced himself. Azam was happy to share more interesting stories over a cup of tea. He took Dante though the collection, explaining the exquisite craftsmanship and the rarity of the products. One discussion led to another and Dante made his second luxe purchase of the day. A golden lighter, Cartier's special edition.

Much later, he realized that he did not smoke. But no worries, it was a day that was special…and unique.

Dante was in love with luxe.

'To rear me was the task of power divine, Supremest wisdom, and primeval love.'

CHAPTER 2

The Power

It was baptism by fire for Dante. His two purchases – which would wipe out a major part of his salary when the credit card bill would be due – had now made him a part of the elite and exclusive clubs of two iconic luxury brands. He was so happy, so engrossed into the two items. He was very eager to show them to Virgil. Moreover, he had two very interesting stories which had given him much food for thought. These stories had opened a new channel to approach luxury…stories. These stories, in most of the cases, were factual, with a dash of fiction and folklore. That's how his quest began in search of stories behind luxe.

Intense research followed and the one that topped his list was of a remarkable and marquee brand – Rolls Royce. He planned to share this story with Virgil over their smoking sessions. Dante was a passive smoker earlier, but the Cartier gold limited edition lighter, he thought, demanded that he started smoking, and an expensive brand at that! Virgil took out his Charminar and before he could take out his match box, Dante quickly lighted it up with his new acquisition. Virgil was taken aback. To his surprise, Dante took out a Marlboro and lighted it up, taking a long and delayed puff. Virgil took the lighter from him and examined it with keen eyes. He was very surprised as the lighter was pretty expensive and he never thought Dante would actually end up buying such an expensive lighter. The game had begun!

Dante smiled and said, "Isn't she a beauty? This was the last piece, made in France." Without further ado, Dante started sharing his story of the Rolls Royce. "You know Virgil, in 1920s, 25% of Rolls Royce sales used to come from India alone. Luxury has a long-lost history with our Royalty. Let me share a story with you about Maharaja Jai Singh of Alwar, who brought this iconic company to its knees.

"He was visiting London. On one of his evening walks in plain English clothes, while passing a Rolls Royce showroom, he decided to go inside and asked the manager about the specifications of the cars, their prices and requested a test drive. The manager just saw an Indian and ignored his request, and went so far as to rudely show the Maharaja the door.

"This treatment naturally made him furious. Jai Singh got back to his hotel and asked for an official visit of the Indian king to the Rolls Royce showroom to be arranged. When he appeared in his formal outfit, dressed in sparkling clothes and jewellery, the Maharaja was welcomed with a red carpet and employees standing on both sides of it paying their respects to the king."

"Jai Singh spent more than two hours in the showroom, trying all the six latest models exhibited. In the end, he purchased all of the cars in the showroom. He paid for them all right away, including the costs of delivery.

"When the cars reached India, he converted them into garbage collectors. This was his revenge. When the word got out, Rolls Royce sent numerous apologies to the Maharaja, but this blemish will stay with Rolls till the brand exists."

Dante took a pause and put out his Marlboro.

While Virgil was listening to this interesting story, his mind and attention was somewhat stuck at the Cartier lighter. He, as editor, had been the sole 'connoisseur' of luxury till now. And while he was using a match, Dante was flaunting a Cartier! "Am I paying him too much?" he wondered to himself.

He did not let it show, but somewhere deep down, he started regretting giving Dante the responsibility of the luxury magazine. He, at some level, did want to expose Dante to luxury and was confident that he would appreciate the world of luxury. But in all this he thought, he being the one to introduce him to this new world, would always remain the last word. He had forgotten that the things he loved about Dante, for which he had trusted him with a new subject and hired him, was his dedication and passion. He consoled himself and thought it might just have been the initial excitement that he took a step forward and actually bought these luxury goods (he had also noticed the LV monogrammed bag by then).

Dante was a keen observer. He did notice a slight change in Virgil's look. He enjoyed the game. These brands made him feel a power that he had never felt before. It was alluring.

*'The mind which is created quick to love,
Is responsive to everything that is pleasing,
Soon as by pleasure it is awakened into activity.'*

CHAPTER 3

The New Identity

Branded luxury gave Dante a new high. With the new-found power, he set sail on a new adventure. Little did he know that his encounter with Virgil was the first step towards 'Limbo', or the first circle of Luxe Inferno. Eight more circles to go till he reaches the centre of the inferno.

The problem with high is that it is addictive. And ironically, plastic money, rather credit card, plays a very significant role.

The trips to the luxury mall became more frequent. In most cases, it was just in search of more stories. And his new friends, the boutique managers, were very happy to see him and chat with him. For them, there were hardly any customers who took interest in the history of these luxury brands. It was always either a hard sale, trying to establish the value for money, or a quick one, wherein the customer exactly knew what he or she wanted and thus made a quick purchase without even exchanging pleasantries. With his exploring new brands, his friend circle also started expanding.

Soon, Dante realized that luxury, especially branded luxury, was an integral part of one's identity. He started noticing brands people around him wore. The watch, the shoes, the jacket, the glasses, the writing instruments, the car... he started closely watching every element of brand presence in an individual. This was a new facet that he had hitherto ignored completely. For Dante, all the other facets still remained important, but somehow, this one started rising the ranks. He soon realized that there are four types of luxury consumers – ranging from a category that shamelessly flaunt the brands to the ones who are very private with their collection. So he decided to write an analysis classifying the consumers in the debut edition of the luxury magazine. Little did he realize how his own identity has transformed and reduced to the brands he used – Cartier lighter, Montblanc pens, Louis Vuitton bags, Gucci glasses, Salvatore Ferragamo shoes, and Armani shirts. Here are some edited excerpts of the debut article:

First, the Experientialists

This genre typically values new and exciting experiences, more than buying products or brands. They lavishly spend on experiences. In their structured lives, they seek a getaway, hence five-star hotel stays, fine dining or adventurous/thrilling experiences are their poison. Luxury to them brings up images of being suspended in time and space, not having the pressures of daily life and work responsibilities as they enjoy the time away.

An exquisite piece of art or a handcrafted timepiece may also give a similar experience when you are just in a space where you are appreciating the beauty of it. It is a time warp; every time you look at it, you become so mesmerised by the beauty that you forget your meetings and deadlines. The experience is the luxury, the experience is the dazzle or luxe.

Personalisation has been able to change the name of the game. So for an experientialist, this personalisation is the value for money.

Personalisation of spending or rather spending on personalisation thus becomes a unique experience.

Now let's meet the Connoisseurs

This genre is passionate in certain areas of interest and is mostly well-informed and knowledgeable about it. These could be art, scotch, wine, watches, writing instruments, cigars, horses, not particularly in that order. These connoisseurs get together and appreciate the finer aspects of their passion. They form clubs and meet for a quiet appreciation of the finer things in life. It may be a Horology Society of time-keepers or a Wine Club or a Cuban Cigar Club or a Super Car Club.

This segment just revels in enjoying what they appreciate the most. For instance, the Single Malt Club members come together, discuss, study, debate and share their appreciation and experience in high spirits (pun intended).

They will spend their time and money in pursuit of the collection of personal passion points. They make the pursuit of their area of passion a mission and pursue it with zest and will not bat an eyelid before spending a fortune on limited editions, or handcrafted editions, or the spirit of the bygone era.

They are reluctant to place value on brands unless it stands for exquisite exclusivity. They take pride in their knowledge of esoteric brands that are not widely known. Luxury to them is purely a matter of the level of craftsmanship, the number of man hours spent, which will determine the quality of the products or services that they buy. Niche, but specialised brands across categories will make their mark with these consumers. They are willing to pay a higher premium, so curated services that bring such products to them will be a great getaway to tap into their need for excellence.

The next segment is the life force that drives luxury in India.

Meet the Flaunters

A socialite friend who used to swear by a clutch that she used to take to every party had secretly confessed that she isn't that fond of it but only carries it for the monogram tag. That's the power of a brand for this category.

Welcome to the world of flaunters, who tend to value brand name over all other factors. The visibility of the brand name at strategic positions across the product is a big deal for them, as such purchases denote their status in their society. So, the brand needs to be aspirational, else, what's the big deal? The newly rich or new money classes, especially their younger counterparts, are mostly badge-seekers at the stage where the brand name is supposedly the biggest status indicator. There is a strong urge to prove to the society that they are also a part of the elitist luxury brand-wagon.

According to a survey, more such consumers were seen in cities like Ludhiana, where they justify the ownership of brands by stating that they are now in a status or position which makes it de rigueur. Interestingly, for this category of consumers, the brands are on a continuum. They can show off Zara as a daily wear to Prada on special occasions with élan.

As flaunters move up the societal ladder, the badge value is conferred not only by the brand, but also by the level of difficulty in obtaining the product or service. Dinner reservation at hard-to-get restaurants, Birkin or Kelly bags for which the wait list is over four years, monogrammed and hot stamped Louis Vuitton bags with their initials, accessories made from exotic leather like of crocodile or snake – the ability to acquire these with relative ease reflects their status.

To tap this segment of consumers, well known but exclusive services and products are the way forward.

And last but not the least, I present to you the Aesthetes

To this category of people, the brand is much less important than the design. Aesthetes are luxury consumers purely because they have arrived at a stage of income due to which they can indulge in their love for design among luxury brands or products. They will shell out a bomb because the object of desire is hand-stitched and not because of the label. They pride themselves for having an eye that picks up the unique and bold in design.

The difference between them and the connoisseur is that the latter has certain passions which they follow with zeal. Quality and craftsmanship are very important for the connoisseurs, however, for the former category, it is the aesthetic appeal, the look, the intricacies of the design that appeal to their senses. They are also likely to pursue this aesthetic across categories, unlike a connoisseur.

Even Aesthetes are Flaunters in a way; they also flaunt their exquisite designs and feel pride at the snob quotient that most people are not even able to understand or appreciate the elegance. They feel exclusive.

*'If the present world goes astray, the cause is in you,
In you it is to be sought.'*

CHAPTER 4

The Clash

So, which category was Dante? Was he a flaunter at heart thinking he was a connoisseur? Or the other way round. There were clearly two levels of his consumption – one was the increasing need for establishing an identity based on branded luxury and the other was purely academic, for the magazine.

While his consumption classification was still a matter of debate, there was one development that he couldn't help but notice – Virgil was slowly but steadily transforming into a 'flaunter' from a 'connoisseur'. Also, every other day, he was busy showing off his 'acquisition' of the latest collection of a luxury brand. A more interesting news came in when one of his friends at the mall told him that Virgil has also enquired about Dante and what he had recently bought.

Dante did not take it well. There was a very wide gap between his and Virgil's salaries. He was in his fifties and Dante was just 27. But Dante was no quitter. He realized it was time to up his game. He needed a new high, beating Virgil in brand one-upmanship. His credit card bills were pinching quite hard, but it was a matter of the three-lettered word that drives luxury – EGO.

So, as per the advice of his relationship manager, he converted the credit card bill into EMIs against a steep monthly interest. And predictably, slowly, the flaunting game turned into a battle. From a buyer of stories, Dante became a "prized patron" of a few luxury brands, so much so, he was offered steady discounts and sneak peeks into private collections of these luxury brands.

His collection swelled and so did his EMIs. Virgil failed to contain his displeasure at being challenged in this luxury flaunting game. No one could remove him from his luxury connoisseur throne, certainly not a 20-something. His anger slipped into the professional arena, and he started venting out his anger on Dante at work, picking on issues just to put him down, show him who was the boss. Virgil had anger management issues and was quite known for his shouting sprees. But Dante, with his newfound power and identity and fully aware of the actual reason behind change in Virgil's behaviour, decided not to back down.

The newsroom witnessed their clashes very frequently. Eventually, every clash boiled down to one question – who was the bigger authority or connoisseur on luxury?

He realized that his salary was not enough as Virgil's war chest was pretty huge. He felt so compelled that even against his wish, just in order to garner borrowed funds from his friends and colleagues, he started lying about his father's health. He hated himself for doing it. He loved his father very much. But this was his last resort. He could not quit the game.

Little did he realize that over the next few months, he would be consumed by his deadly sins and would slowly move deeper from Upper Hell to Lower Hell, steadily running towards the 9th or innermost circle.

*'O human race, born to fly upward,
wherefore at a little wind dost thou so fall?'*

CHAPTER 5

To Hell and Back

One year passed by; Dante and Virgil's one-upmanship game only increased its intensity. It had grown from brands to the latest collections of the same brands. Dante was completely hooked on to the game, its addiction, and was enjoying it thoroughly. His status in the organization had also elevated as he was directly pitted against the Editor-in-Chief. Another bone of contention was the fact that in lieu of his day-to-day writings on luxury brands, he had to meet many CXOs of these luxury brands, which increased his network as well as knowledge of these brands and also resulted in invitations to visit their headquarters in Switzerland or Dubai. These interactions helped him get a deeper insight into the brand story, which he later penned down in his book. So, to these luxury brand CXOs, Dante became the face of the paper, and not Virgil.

Even with the rising clashes and credit card dues as well as borrowings, life was good. Dante was moving from one high to another. He was totally consumed by the addiction.

But one phone call changed everything. His father was diagnosed with cancer at an Advanced stage.

There was a sudden need for cash, as then cancer was not covered under the company's insurance policy. He was earning very decently and could have saved enough for an emergency even after continuing his existing standard of living. The keyword is "could have" because he "could not". His savings were zilch, rather negative. All he had were 10 wallets, 12 slings, 8 watches, 15 writing instruments and the list went on.

If you calculate the total money spent on these labels, it could jolly well take care of the medical expense. But these were of no use now. Just no use at all. The worst hit was when he realized that his EMI was consuming more than half his salary. And there was no asset against it, neither a house nor a car, which he could sell off.

He was completely helpless with the credit card EMIs and the money borrowed. He had no idea from where he would get the money to treat his ailing father.

A sudden realization dawned on him. What was the point of all this? It was just a game of one-upmanship that led to this disaster. From an upstart journalist, today he stood almost a pauper where his greed had made him incapable of supporting his father during this time of need.

He cursed the day he had first borrowed money from his close friend Suresh, citing his father's ill-health as an excuse. He could not forgive himself for that. Was it bad karma and was his father was paying the price?

He realized he was in the centre of Luxe Inferno where the Devil himself resides.

He had committed treason against his father with the lie.

He needed to come back from this hell and help his dying father or kill himself in this inferno.

All this while, he was justifying his addiction with academic interest. He loved the subject, but the seven sins took him to the dark side of luxe, inside this rabbit hole. Now, he regretted his addiction, he regretted his entire journey through the nine circles of the inferno.

But he had to come back; he had to come back for his father.

*'Consider your origin.
You were not formed to live like brutes
but to follow virtue and knowledge.'*

CHAPTER 6

The Paradiso

Luxury is just like science or technology; it is as good and as bad as the user makes of it. If the sins of humans decide to take luxury to the bottomless pit of hell, it is very easy. It is also easy to enjoy the subject and the learnings and not be addicted to it, not to identify with it. Once the latter approach is taken, we realize that luxury – or rather branded luxury – is not who we are; it is not our identity, it is what dream merchants want us to believe. The essence of luxury needs to be savoured slowly, enjoyed like a good book or like a memorable journey, and all the while keeping your identity intact.

Dante knew that his addiction was supported by two things which needed to be severed immediately – Virgil and his one-upmanship with him, as well as the city that hailed this blatant showcasing and flaunting of luxury brands.

The next morning, he bid Virgil goodbye, quit the job and the city for good, to be with his father. He quit the game. In the next few weeks, he managed to sell most of his prized possessions and pay his debt. It was his moment of clarity, his nirvana.

On the other hand, Virgil was relieved that he would again reclaim his title as the luxury connoisseur. A part of him, however, missed Dante and the game, especially the adrenaline rush. But very soon he found a new Dante and continued a new game with her. To Virgil, the inferno was an infinite loop from which he could never transcend.

The journey to hell and back had given Dante a perspective of luxe and luxury that was rare and had put him in a very advantageous position as a writer. He decided to pen his thoughts and perspectives and take it to a wider audience so that people could understand luxury beyond the "price tag". He started writing columns on luxury for a few foreign publications and sharing his ideas in various forums, which helped him take care of the expenses of his father's cancer treatment. Dante realized luxury was a much wider subject and to understand it one needed to understand both the dazzle and the darkness that hides behind it.

One day, when he was telling his father how this one-upmanship has dearly cost him as well as Virgil, Dante's father laughed and narrated a story. He said, during the time of Zamindars in Bengal, one-upmanship was very common. There were two neighbouring Zamindars who were almost at war with each other over this never-ending competition – who is superior. So, when one day Zamindar A purchased and showcased his new imported two-horse driven Phaeton, Zamindar B got jealous. Within a week, he bought and showcased a four-horse driven imported Phaeton. A got very jealous and increased the number of horses by two, B retaliated by increasing it further. A took a step forward and replaced the horses by two zebras. This was the first zebra-driven Phaeton in Calcutta. They both laughed and the story helped Dante unburden his guilt a bit.

A year had passed, but his father's condition had still not improved. For over a year, he had not made any luxury purchase. He had sold most of his luxury belongings and even gave away a few to his friends.

His writings were well accepted by audience and looked beyond any myopic view of luxury, tracing its evolution and how it has manifested itself in today's world.

The moment he ceased being a luxe-o-holic, freeing himself from the addiction, he fell in love with luxe.

The purgatory of life had made him live with death and a fear of losing his father to a deadly disease every moment, regretting his journey to Luxe Inferno.

One day when the doctor told him that the final days of his father were nearing, Dante broke into tears. His father was a strong man. He told him, "Son, life is short, and I have lived a full life. I have no regrets as I have you by my side. I want you to understand that every experience – good or bad – was God's way of teaching you to pass in this exam called life. His objective is not to kill you, but to make you stronger. So, your experience with luxury and the sins which took you to hell and back was necessary. Life has been your purgatory, and you are now wiser and stronger. It has given you a purpose. So always know that God has been very kind and thank him."

After a few days, his father passed away. He tried to remain strong but broke down into tears intermittently. He was not able to contain his emotions. The loss was unbearable. It was a very deep wound, a gift from his inferno, which changed something deep within him. It was a throbbing pain. Unbearable. Intermittently, he felt the urge to relieve himself of this pain, to liberate the wound. To accept that change and liberate himself. He had picked up the razor a few times, taken it close to his wrist, made the cold steel touch the vein and feel the throbbing pulse. More than once, he had been convinced this was the only way to relieve himself of the pain, to escape this hell, to purgate himself. His sins took away his father. He could never forgive himself.

But then, he could hear his father's last words, "…life has been your purgatory and you are now wiser and stronger."

Dante has to rise from his ashes like a phoenix, for his father's sake.

Would the Luxe Inferno ever set him free?

Would he ever see the Paradiso?

'Into the eternal darkness, into fire and into ice.'

Part B
Perception

CHAPTER 1

Musings of millennial millionaires

Did Rolex ever fathom their biggest competition will be a technology giant – Apple. Smartwatches by Cupertino, a California-based company have become the biggest threat to the legendary Swiss watchmaker.

And lo and behold, they have even come up with solid gold versions to bring the price range in direct competition to Rolex. It is the best of technology and luxe on your wrist.

How times are changing! When the pace and preferences of tech-tuned, temperamental millennials are forcing businesses to be on tenterhooks, can luxury behemoths ignore this dynamic generation?

There is an entirely new category of customers that are added to the existing classification of Experientialists, Connoisseurs, Flaunters and Aesthetes – make way for the millennial millionaires!

It is an entirely new category of buyers with a very different perception of luxury. These are the second or third generation Richie Rich with a spending capacity similar to affluent Baby boomers or Generation X.

Luxe custodians need to now pay close attention to the musings of these millennial millionaires.

The biggest challenge is that their worldview is not the same as their fathers' or grandfathers'. No wonder, Rolex is losing millions of potential customers to Apple. So how can luxury brands woo this new set of trailblazing consumers?

Decoding millennial millionaires: All luxury brands need to do a deep dive into the lives of these millennials to understand their choices and preferences. The objective of this customer immersion is to understand a very fundamental question – what dazzles them? 'Old wine in a new bottle' strategy will work for them. What has historically worked, will work no more. Some characteristics of these millennial millionaires are:

- In today's connected world, they know the latest trends in luxury, fashion and technology across the globe.

- They are impatient, so they need to be convinced very quickly.

- They are very demanding customers and will always want their preferred product yesterday. So they need to be handled with care.

- They are impulsive buyers, so all brands need to have a deep understanding of using this impulse for their benefit, especially in their marketing strategy.

- They will not bat an eyelid before changing their preferred brand. So never take brand loyalty for granted.

- Luxury brands have to bring in a "cool" quotient to woo them. Traditional excellence will not work well.

Preference for digital media: This generation lives with latest technology and mostly in a virtual world. This is a boon and a bane for luxe. Earlier, there was a huge issue of suitable and prime real estate for these luxury brands to set shop. These needed to be in the crème-de-la-crème locations to woo the so-called New Maharajas and give them a royal experience. But getting such real estate was becoming a huge problem, both in terms of availability and cost, for all these brands across the globe. Today, with the advent of e-marketplaces, this problem is resolved. Millennials prefer their luxury shopping online, and not offline. Ironically, solutions often come with problems. E-commerce has given an enormous boost to the counterfeit industry wherein hundreds of new websites have popped up, showcasing pics of original luxury goods being sold at heavy discounts of up to 80%. Most millennials are not even aware that they are buying fakes.

New-age ads: Marketing luxury has always been a challenge as the objective always is to create a sense of aspiration and exclusivity. Inspiring personalities who have created a legacy were the first choices as brand ambassadors or representatives of the brands, such as JFK for Rolex. Niche magazines were identified wherein advertisements were given. These two very potent ways of advertising fall flat as far as these millionaire millennials are concerned. Therefore, new models need to be identified – personalities who are "cool" and "inspiring". The choice of advertising media also needs to be changed to include a heavy dose of digital and social media. The millennials prefer videos to print advertisements, and their attention span is reduced to seconds. Therefore, all luxury marketers have to invest in new-age campaigns through the right media with loads of "cool" quotient to woo these millennial millionaires. Instagram and Snapchat are more relevant than a Forbes or a Fortune.

Tech Talk: This by far is the biggest threat. As stated earlier, the way Apple is eating into Rolex's market, all luxury brands need to be careful from not only their immediate competitors, but also these tech companies. These millennial millionaires swear by technology, and thus, the latest in technology carries the most "cool" quotient. All luxury brands need to keep an eye on the latest technology trends and products that lure these millennials and shape their strategy accordingly.

CHAPTER 2

Masstige – Luxury of the Masses

The essence of a luxury brand lies in the exclusivity it offers. While this exclusivity subtly opens its doors to moolah, unfortunately, it does not necessarily keep counters ringing for all.

Thus, as a survival strategy, all luxury brands owe their existence to a very special category – the masstige. A portmanteau of the words 'mass' and 'prestige', 'masstige' has been described as 'prestige for the masses'. The term was popularised by Michael Silverstein and Neil Fiske in their book *Trading Up* and a Harvard Business Review article titled 'Luxury for the Masses'.

Masstige products are defined as "premium but attainable," and have two aspects: (1) They are considered luxury or premium products, and (2) They have price points that fill the gap between mid-market and super premium.

Luxury has indeed become a volume game with the great Indian middle class, leading the luxe game from the front.

Let's take the example of Louis Vuitton's Speedy 30 handbag, which has been nicknamed the three-second bag in Korea because it feels like you see one every three seconds. As one of the many entry-level products, this has been developed to deliver value for money on a smaller, yet perhaps equally indulgent taste of the brand narrative. So, entry-level products – accessories, belts, scarves, wallets, small purses, and the likes – of the luxury brands have a clear demand among this segment. They cater to the need of just flaunting the labels.

While exclusivity remains the key element, all luxury brands extend downwards with these low-hanging, seemingly-affordable fruits to whet the appetite of the value-for-label masses. Today, masstige products have democratised luxury and made it accessible to both the *raja* (the king) and the *praja* (the subjects) alike.

Another key advantage of masstige is that it keeps counterfeits and first copies at bay. The members of the great Indian middle class are logo-conscious and yet feel a little pang when they have to shell out a bomb to flaunt a luxury brand. At the same time, they also feel guilty when they choose to use luxury counterfeits for satiating their need to flaunt luxury. However, thanks to the masstige products, this multi-billion-dollar counterfeit market takes a hit. With scarfs, belts, coin purses, perfumes of the luxury brands being available at prices, which to the price-sensitive Indian buyers are worth the logo, they end up moving away from buying counterfeits and first copies.

But, what if this greed for the bottomline from masstige steals the luxury brand's exclusivity quotient? To what extent can the brand be diluted without taking a hit? In my book *Decoding Luxe* I have formulated a three-part solution on how luxury brands can get the right mix of their products, without diluting the brand and keeping the moolah flowing:

1. A brand needs to identify its signature products and add a premium to the prices. These are meant to tease the aspirations of the GIMC, who can't afford them. Mostly display the pictures of these signature items, making sure they are always out of stock, with fresh stock on the anvil from Germany or France. The GIMC is sure to keep coming back.

2. A brand needs to identify special edition, handcrafted pieces that it wants the Richie Rich to buy. These should be on display so that the Richie Rich can get a feel of the product,

and then take it home, just a like a piece of history. These have a premium attached due to their exclusivity.

3. And finally comes the masstige products to satiate the appetite of the GIMC for them to flaunt that logo of the brand they always aspired to buy.

CHAPTER 3

Of Flaunters and Bling Economy

For luxury brands, all that glitters is gold. Bling is a tried and tested strategy to attain glittering success.

To understand this better, let me first take you through the mindset of luxury consumers. As stated earlier, there are four categories in which I have classified luxury buyers globally in my book *Decoding Luxe*. They are Experientialists, Connoisseurs, Aesthetes and Flaunters.

Flaunters tend to value brand name over all other factors. Purchase of a brand is a symbol of their status in society. The visibility of the brand name is important. It is also important for the brand to be aspirational, otherwise, what's the big deal? Badge seekers are mostly the neo-rich and young, having a strong desire to prove to the society that they have jumped aboard the elitist, luxury brand-wagon. They are driving luxury in India. And this is the category of logo seekers and flaunters to whom the bling appeals the most.

There are distinctly two categories of luxury brands – One goes all out to scream the bling; the other stays muted in its appeal to be classy. Let me elaborate a bit.

Consider Louis Vuitton. The brand has since inception believed in being the flaunter's favourite. If you look at old Bond movies, from luggage to briefcase to chequebook covers to files, every leather accessory will carry the LV monogram. LV is historically designed in such a way that the brand is evident from a distance. A similar brand philosophy is with Rolex. The bling is an integral part of its brand philosophy.

No wonder, the two most trusted brands for the flaunters, including the debonair British spy James Bond, since time immemorial have been Louis Vuitton and Rolex.

On the other extreme lie brands that prefer to be muted in their bling quotient as they prefer to attract the categories of connoisseurs and aesthetes, and not the flaunters. Examples are Montblanc and Bottega Veneta. While the former decided to be muted as writing instruments are meant to exude a sense of dignity and class, the latter's motto is "when your own initials are enough". So rather than having a logo, Bottega Veneta chose to celebrate Brand "you". In a way, even Rolls Royce has a similar sentiment; RR logo is enough and does not cater to the flaunter category. I am not considering the diamond-studded, solid gold, custom-made ones. For these brands, it is all about class, which the bling takes away.

And then with time, these classy brands realised that the demographic of the customers is shifting from 40-plus to 20-plus. Hip-hop stars who epitomise the bling in luxury are becoming icons and driving their sales. Rolls Royce tried to take on blingy and flashy Ferrari by entering sports car segment; Montblanc launched a new collection with "MB" monogram, and so on.

The world of luxury is slowly and steadily getting caught in the bling economy.

CHAPTER 4

Art of Subliminal Marketing

Getting loud and on the face is the primary mantra for luxury branding. However, there is a relatively small, albeit growing and loyal segment which still believes in a subliminal appeal of luxury. Branding to them is very difficult and thus, an art. They loathe brands which do not have class and go all out to showcase their products in the most brazen way. They loathe the brands which are popular with customers who are flaunters. 'Money can't buy you class', that is the moot point that drives this genre of customers. For a better understanding of subtle and subliminal branding, let us first understand the buyer categories that need to be lured in – Connoisseurs and Aesthetes.

Let's first meet the Connoisseurs. This genre is passionate in certain areas of interest and makes it a point to be well-informed and knowledgeable about it. These categories could be art, scotch, wine, watches, writing instruments, cigars, horses, and the likes. These connoisseurs get together and appreciate the finer aspects of their passion. They look down upon people who do not share their passion. They form clubs and get together for a quiet appreciation of luxury of creation. It may be a horology society or a wine club or a scotch club or a cigar group. Being rich is a necessary but certainly not the sufficient condition for being a part of this exclusive group of connoisseurs. You need to belong to a certain class to be a part of this group.

They will spend their time and money in pursuit of the collection of personal passion points. They make the pursuit of their area of passion a mission and pursue it with zest. When it comes to limited editions, or handcrafted editions or spirit of the bygone era, these connoisseurs will not bat an eyelid before spending a fortune.

And then come the Aesthetes. To this genre, the brand is much less important than the design. Aesthetes are luxury consumers purely because they have arrived at a state of income due to which they can indulge in their love for design among luxury brands or products. They will shell out a bomb because the object of desire is hand-stitched and not because of the label. They pride themselves for having an eye that picks out the unique and bold in design. Again, money or the brazen display of affluence is frowned upon by this category of buyers. They are more into the appreciation of finer things in life, and money surely can't develop that faculty.

The difference between them and the connoisseur is that the latter has certain passions which they follow with zeal and the quality and craftsmanship are very important. However, for the former category, it is the aesthetic appeal, the look, the intricacies of the design that appeal to their senses. They are also likely to pursue this aesthetic across categories, unlike a connoisseur. Thus comes the art of subliminal marketing, which is the key for engaging both these customer categories. Brands need to focus on the story, the creativity and the uniqueness of a product and certainly not on the price point. It is very difficult to lure these two categories with the usual razzle dazzle that works for the majority of customers. On the contrary, bling drives these customers away from a brand. They are a serious lot, who has the potential of being loyal as well as brand ambassadors, spreading the good word. The key to make these two categories loosen their purse strings is to be subliminal and low key.

These customers usually come from old money and thus are not dazzled by luxury or rather price tags. They look for something unique in the product, so the branding has to be specific to showcasing the uniqueness of it. The brand story has to be told in a manner that attracts the interest of these Connoisseurs and Aesthetes. Be it the uniqueness of the design or the man hours spent by a master craftsman or the rarity of the raw material, the brand story has to appeal at a subliminal level.

For example, a rare brand of shawl Shahtoosh, meaning King of Wools, is now a banned item. It uses the wool from a rare Tibetan antelope. Master artisans weaved delicate hair, which measured between 7 and 10 microns, to make these shawls so fine that they can be passed through a wedding ring. The mere collection of wools from these migratory animals moving down from Mongolia to Tibet takes years. The branding of Shahtoosh, thus will have to be on the rarity and not on the price tag to appeal at a subliminal level.

CHAPTER 5

Darkness behind the veil of luxury

Luxury has always been for the chosen few, exclusive. Luxury creates a great divide between the haves and have-nots. You either have it or you don't; or rather, you can either afford it, or you can't. Luxury has its origin in the word luxe, which means dazzle. So, whenever you think of luxury, it is always about razzle-dazzle, it is always about glam and glitz. The stuff dreams are made of. Dreams that only the chosen few can buy. And every bit of luxury exudes a shine that blinds the have-nots. Sorry Mr Marx, this is not the world of the Proletariats.

Behind this razzle-dazzle, there is another life… A life as real as that of the have-nots… a life filled with lust, hatred, jealousy, anger… a life very deprived, very starved… a life of horrors… a life of flesh and blood… But yes, a life to die for, or rather kill!

Luxury remains a silent witness to that darkness.

This is a side that existed since the genesis of luxe, just like the dark side of the moon.

Luxury's dazzle paves way for the deadly sins and ego, which soon tear apart every moral fabric. In the core of luxe lies a sense of exclusivity, entitlement and this makes you feel above the cattle class, above the have-nots.

The darkness that hides behind the dazzle of luxury mostly remains secret; some even become folklore – either of royalty or corporate.

Let me share a folklore of a certain Maharaja who was snubbed by a Brit salesman in London at a Rolls-Royce store as he failed to recognise him and treated the Maharaja as an ordinary poor Indian. The Maharaja was shown the door. The Maharaja could not take the insult and returned the next day in his royal attire and bought all the six Phantoms, to be shipped to his kingdom. His ego was so hurt that just buying all the Phantoms in the showroom was not enough to soothe it. Once the Phantoms reached his kingdom, he ordered that they need to be decorated befitting their royalty. And then, he ordered these Phantoms to be used for collecting garbage, day after day. Rolls-Royce Phantom is a car that proverbially "runs on reputation", so the news spread like wildfire and caused a large dent in the revenues of the luxury car maker. The reputation was at stake. The Maharaja's ego was finally soothed. In one story in my book *Dark Luxe*, I have taken a creative liberty giving a Phantom a mind of its own, creating a 'what if' moment on revenge for reputation.

Then there are folklores of certain priceless gems that were responsible for writing the history of empires in blood.

Coming to a more known ground and its lesser-known darkness – the corporate tales of blood and gore. Espionage is a very common phenomenon, and luxury and fashion houses are no stranger to it. There are horror stories of usurping designs and ideas by rival houses and then going to extents that will make even Dante contemplate a new Inferno. Last year, a headline hit the fashion world with French fashion house Saint Laurent Paris (YSL) being accused of copying a design of a clutch bag in Fall 2017 runway show at Paris Fashion Week. It was alleged to be a mirror image of the Mburu bag designed by Senegalese brand, Tongoro collection, launched by Sarah Diouf.

Earlier this year, this paper reported a story of a Delhi-based brand, People Tree, making allegations against Christian Dior after seeing their block prints on the cover of a magazine. "Featuring on the cover of *Elle* magazine, Sonam Kapoor was seen adorned in a boho-chic dress with the controversial print. The vibrant dress in the rustic shade was paired with a frilled multi-coloured patchwork shrug. While initially, it garnered a positive response, later, allegations of 'blatant plagiarism' made the dress and its designer, Christian Dior, an internet buzz."

Luxury remains a constant lure, giving people a justification to go deep into the bottomless pits of hell. All these stories are guarded with life. But some spill over into nasty legal battles.

With the steady rise of consumerism, it is only fair to assume that luxe will remain the strongest lure for both the haves and have-nots, either the desire to remain exclusive or the desire to become one, and thus both can be pushed to the dark side.

CHAPTER 6

Of aspirations and mind games

What lies at the core of luxe is a deep desire. What drives luxe is again a deep desire. In the course of branding or marketing luxury, what we actually do is brand and market desire. Desire, however, is tricky. Because just like a human heart, it can swing both ways, taking luxe along with it, to both extremes. So, like the age-old cassettes, there are two sides of it – Side A and Side B.

Side A: This one will be the positive side, which leads to aspirations. This is the side that keeps the fire of aspirations burning in the human hearts and thus counters ringing for luxury brands. This is the desire that keeps you awake at nights and makes you chase your dreams of dazzle.

Imagine this, you love fast cars and finally have stretched your budget to acquire your dream car - a BMW Z4. You have fulfilled your desire to drive the meanest machine in town. While driving your brand-new dream car, say on the fifth day, suddenly, a Ferrari 812 Superfast zips past you. As a car enthusiast, you are well aware of the model and you know it is priced way beyond your budget, even in foreseeable future, at over five crore rupees. And you are a practical woman. Till the time you had only seen its photograph and it was fine to go for Z4. But the moment you see it in front of your eyes, something changed. In no time, you realise that your desire has a sudden change of heart. The Z4 has been removed from the throne of your dream car and replaced by 812 Superfast. You save a photograph of your new dream car on your phone, so that you can inspire yourself every day to own this new machine… as soon as possible.

In this way, desire helps you rise the ladder of luxury and so brand custodians or dream merchants are very quick to manipulate your desires so that they can achieve their targets. You need to understand that the dream merchants, while selling you the dream car, will make sure that there is a practical picture painted, so that in the quest of upgrading directly to 812 Superfast, you don't skip the intermediate step and not buy the Z4. They will make sure that they make you desire for both and also desire an upgrade immediately after you make the purchase. Thus, desires in the positive form of aspirations fuel the luxury industry.

Side B: Desire can also swing towards bottomless pits of hell and take luxury along with it. In my second book of the Luxe Trilogy, *Dark Luxe*, I have explored in detail the second aspect of desire. This is the story of nightmares, about those realities that safely hide behind the veil of luxe. These are tales of fiction from the darkest pits of hell.

There are examples from life where luxury is made an accomplice to achieve the deepest and darkest desires. These are not aspirations; these are manifestations of the seven deadly sins and how desire makes luxe an integral part of it.

Let me elaborate with a story from *Dark Luxe*. This is a story of a golden pair of scissors which the younger brother uses to kill the Maharaja so that he can take over the throne. The significance of this pair is that these are the sharpest pair made of pure gold and was historically used to severe the placenta, separating a new born royal from the mother. The caveat is that this ritual is meant only for the first born, the one who is entitled to the throne. Sheer jealousy and desire for the throne made the brother kill his brother with the same pair of scissors, which had given him his identity as the heir to the throne.

Desire creates the darkest secrets, safely hidden in the corridors of power and luxury, and stays silent as a witness. Thus, branding desire is the elixir that a dream merchant aims to capture to brand the ultimate luxe.

CHAPTER 7

Discovering facets of Luxe Identity

What's an identity? May be our name, our gender, our profession, our family, things that define us. Isn't it? If we look at it spiritually, even these are not your identity; it is much deeper, known as your "original face" which you can only see once you go beyond these elements that you think define you.

A luxe brand also has an identity. It also has a gender, a family, and other elements that define it. Gender? Yes, let me explain. When you think of Rolex, is it historically a male brand. If you trace its historic advertising campaigns and brand ambassadors such as "Live for Greatness", which features JFK and Martin Luther King Jr. The brand is essentially an extension of the male identity.

An exclusive watch brand Patek Phillipe has an iconic ad campaign that recently completed twenty years, "You never actually own a Patek Philippe. You merely look after it for the next generation." A Patek watch isn't a device for telling time. It's an heirloom that transfers values across generations. Now if you closely look at the visuals, they are a father-son duo. It is only after much criticism of their gender bias that they decided to come up with a visual with a girl and her mother. But essentially, they focused singularly on the male identity of the watch.

There are two aspects of identity, just like our life. One is internal, what a brand thinks or oneself and the other is external, what consumers think of the brand.

The external identity becomes the real identity that matters at the end of the day. For example, a Patek can charge USD 2.5 million for a timepiece. Now internally, it may think that this price is justified, given the identity of Patek as an heirloom. Now in commerce, this identity will not matter. The identity that will matter is what its consumers think it is really worth. If there are no buyers at this price, then Patek's internal brand identity is not in line with the ground reality. Thus, it warrants a serious course correction, which means a relook at the areas where the company needs to wake up and smell the coffee, thus, to strategize how it can elevate the external identity to the aspired level.

And always, the market acts as a great leveller and is quick to tell a brand what it is worth. Then the brand needs to look into various facets to figure the way forward. A brand can choose one of the three strategies:

1. The brand stays arrogant and ignores the market signal completely.

2. The brand bows to the market pressure and revisits its pricing and corrects it.

3. The brand internally is confident of its worth and thus knows that the price is right, but it is not arrogant and respects the market. So, it understands that the need of the hour is to strategize towards making the brand's external identity more exquisite.

While the first group loses the battle in no time, the second group is smart and wins the short-term battle. The third group, however, is the prudent one which wins the long-term battle. Market indicators are like an "acid test" for the brand's identity and its worth. These inputs need to be taken very seriously if the brand wants to survive the test of time. The brand needs to build its external identity, giving a hard look at various facets – including the way boutique managers are handling customers, post-sale customer service as well a brand campaign, or the selection of brand ambassadors.

It is the marriage of the external and internal identities that make a luxury brand stand the test of time.

CHAPTER 8

The Luxe Legacy

The key to creating luxe is 'aspiration'. Brand custodians have one, all-focussed task at hand – to create aspiration. The craving of a consumer to be associated with a brand is the key to his wallet or her purse. And 'brand legacy' is a fail-safe mechanism for creating desire and dazzle.

Legacy typically means 'inheritance', something passed on from one generation to next. There is a sense of exclusivity to the whole notion of legacy. This exclusivity and a desire to belong to a certain legacy give the opportunity to a brand to create an 'aspirational quotient'.

Imagine yourself using a luggage brand that was once exclusively used by the Maharajas. Or imagine wearing a watch brand that was worn by legendary leaders such as JFK. You feel that a part of you is connected to that legacy that has a high 'aspirational quotient'. It is almost as if the earlier generation of royalty or legends have passed on to your generation, to you. Such is the high of exclusivity, in turn, establishing an instant connect of the brand with the consumer.

Talking of royalties, let me elaborate with an example of the palaces. Let's take the case of the beautiful and exquisite Lake Palace, which is now with Taj Lake Palace Udaipur. With its guest list including Queen Elizabeth, former first lady Jacqueline Kennedy, Shah of Iran, Lord Kurzon and Vivian Leigh, it is no wonder that they charge 20,000 USD per night on average. Or take the example of the Raj Palace of Jaipur, which charges a tariff as high as 50,000 USD. Royal Suite of

Raj Palace is the second-most expensive suite in the world. Now these are real palaces, which companies have converted into hotels.

The service in these 'palace hotels' is aligned to the service that Maharajas used to receive. Once you spend time in these palaces and drink from a gold glass, or eat from a gold plate, or admire the real gold used in decorating a wall, the entire ambiance is created, may be overdone, in such a way to dazzle you and make you feel 'privileged' in the company of royalty. Soon you realize that you are really living a life of a Maharaja, and it does not require any bloodline anymore. It is like an inheritance, a legacy. These hotels thrive on the aspirational quotient and thus essentially on legacy of the 'Brand Royalty'.

Now, will a seasoned hotel brand like Taj be able to charge the same premium by 'creating a palace'? The answer is no. The reason being a lack of history. The fact that these 'palaces' have a history and thus a legacy, already nudges the consumers to loosen their purse strings. What adds to the premium is the way royalty is showcased with the opulence to recreate the times of the Maharajas.

Watch brands like IWC also boast of Presidents wearing their watch and thus of legacy. However, Rolex takes the cake here. The former being more exclusive and Rolex being more inclusive, the appeal of legacy of Rolex reaches far and wide. And so, it can easily accommodate a Roger Federer in the "Live for Greatness" campaign along with JFK and Martin Luther King Jr.

Thus, a brand custodian needs to evaluate the brand and understand how a legacy needs to be marketed well so that it does not end up alienating people. If a group of potential buyers are not encouraged to be a part of the legacy of JFK, they might fall for Federer.

Let your quest for luxe legacy continue.

CHAPTER 9

Philosophy behind Branding Desire

When you hear the name of a particular luxury brand, what is the first thought? The answer is, it depends. The images that are already conjured by the custodians, who brand desire as well as your personal experiences with the brand, are responsible for bringing up these first thoughts. So, in one part, it is the real experience, and on the other, the imaginative faculty that the brand can successfully arouse. In this mix of fact and fiction, what really transpires is very personal. If your experience is good or if it had left a sour taste will finally determine the outcome. On the surface, every luxury brand aims to give a sense of exclusivity and class. It is a tool to make you feel special. And the premium charged is just a means to an end.

What exactly is the philosophy behind branding desire? Essentially it means the promise that a brand makes to its customers. Let me explore some facets of brand philosophy:

Brand existence: The first critical piece behind brand philosophy is the prime reason behind its existence, the raison d'être. Why do we need that brand in an already cluttered brand-verse? The brand needs to find the reason of its existence and establish it in the eyes of the customers.

Brand positioning: After establishing its reason for existence, and once the brand itself is convinced on its existence, it is time to find a niche and establish itself in the eyes of its customers. So now, from the brand's eyes to the customer's eyes, the brand is finally able to establish its niche.

Brand story: The third component of the philosophy is the brand story. This is the time when the custodians have their creative juices flowing. This is the best way to establish the brand philosophy to the customers. For example, if the brand philosophy is to live the core values, then the story has to be built around how the brand actually is walking the talk and not just doing lip service. The brand campaigns, which are used to tell this story, have to be clear in their narrative as to how a brand is living up to its philosophy.

Brand communication: Taking the story across various media helps communicate the brand story to the target audience. A brand needs to identify the right format and the right media for communicating its story to establish its philosophy. For example, if a luxury brand wants to reach out to a young audience, then the preferred format will be videos as opposed to a print ad, which is more suited for a more mature clientele. Similarly, the media chosen for a young audience will be social media versus a magazine for more mature clients. These choices are the reasons why communication is impactful, or it fails to resonate with the audience.

Brand touch points: No matter how successfully a brand is able to communicate its philosophy, sloppy handling of a client can make or break its reputation. Be it an inappropriate gesture at a boutique by a rookie or by an over-smart manager, or even a rude customer care executive over a phone call, it will do more harm than a brand custodian can ever imagine. It is the 'fact' that I was talking about, that with the sprinkled 'fiction', will conjure up the real philosophy in the minds of the customers.

*'Lost are we, and are only so far punished,
That without hope we live on in desire.'*

Part C

Epilogue

An ode to Darkness

I had a dream, which was not all a dream.
The bright sun was extinguish'd, and the stars
Did wander darkling in the eternal space,
Rayless, and pathless, and the icy earth
Swung blind and blackening in the moonless air;
Morn came and went—and came, and brought no day,
And men forgot their passions in the dread
Of this their desolation; and all hearts
Were chill'd into a selfish prayer for light:
And they did live by watchfires—and the thrones,
The palaces of crowned kings—the huts,
The habitations of all things which dwell,
Were burnt for beacons; cities were consum'd,
And men were gather'd round their blazing homes
To look once more into each other's face;

--Darkness by Lord Byron

It was during a trip through the dark catacombs of St. Stephen's Cathedral in Vienna that a thought dawned on me. The Stephen's Cathedral hosts the tombs of Prince Eugene of Savoy (PES), commander of the Imperial forces during the War of the Spanish Succession in the Chapel of The Cross (northwest corner of the cathedral) and of Frederick III, Holy Roman Emperor (Fr3), under whose reign the Diocese of Vienna was canonically erected on 18 January 1469, in the Apostles' Choir (southeast corner of the cathedral). The basement of the cathedral also hosts the Bishops, Provosts and Ducal crypts. The most recent interment in the Bishop's crypt completed in 1952 under the south choir was that of 98-year-old Cardinal Franz König in 2004. Provosts of the cathedral are buried in another chamber.

When you see the seemingly innocent urns little would you know what it contains. The Ducal Crypt located under the chancel holds 78 bronze containers with the bodies, hearts, or viscera of 72 members of the Habsburg dynasty. Before his death in 1365, Duke Rudolf IV ordered the crypt built for his remains in the new cathedral he commissioned. By 1754, the small rectangular chamber was overcrowded with 12 sarcophagi and 39 urns, so the area was expanded with an oval chamber added to the east end of the rectangular one. In 1956, the two chambers were renovated and their contents rearranged. The sarcophagi of Duke Rudolf IV and his wife were placed upon a pedestal and the 62 urns containing organs were moved from the two rows of shelves around the new chamber to cabinets in the original one.

This was history, courtesy the cathedral guide, but here is the interesting bit...When the charnel house and eight cemeteries abutting the cathedral's side and back walls closed due to an outbreak of bubonic plague in 1735, the bones within them were moved to the catacombs below the church. Burials directly in the catacombs occurred until 1783, when a new law forbade most burials within the city.

It was very cold inside the catacombs, you will get an eerie feeling, a feeling of some presence. Suddenly my curiosity made me peep through a window into a dimly lit room. My blood cuddled and a chill ran through my spines. Yes, I am using clichés, as sometimes they best describe your feelings. It was a room of death. Human bones and skulls were stacked neatly in the room. And then this was only one of the rooms – the rooms of death. The remains of over 11,000 persons are in the catacombs – just their bones and skulls.

After gaining back my stupor, I looked into the next room and then the next – no glass barriers, only a window. After a few windows and innovative patterns with which human bones and skulls can be stacked, I felt nauseated.

It was at that moment this thought dawned on me -- have I given the readers a similar experience?

Are my stories like these rooms of death interspersed with flashes of dazzle?

Maybe, maybe not. But that is for my readers to let me know.

Like the walls of the catacomb, luxury remains a silent witness.

Let your quest for luxury continue, even if it has to pass through the nine circles of Inferno!

www.ingramcontent.com/pod-product-compliance
Lightning Source LLC
LaVergne TN
LVHW091538070526
838199LV00002B/114